Praise for
Why Intolerance and Extremism Happen

"This is a book for any common-sense person who has looked around at the political division and outrage-fueled information environment and said, 'What the hell is going on?' or 'How did we get here?'"
—Dannagal Young, Professor of Communication and Political Science at the University of Delaware

"Kanefield synthesizes insights from prominent scholars across different academic fields to give us a deeper understanding of how we got here. A brilliant book that everyone should read."
—Peter Arenella, UCLA Law Professor Emeritus

"Kanefield brings her extraordinary intellect and insight to bear on the question of how humans might live in peace with one another. Combining this with her superpower of conveying, clearly and simply, very complex ideas, Kanefield has produced a concise but masterful guide to why things have gone awry in this era of polarization—and how we might find our way back. I could not recommend it more highly."
—Karen Stenner, political and behavioral scientist and author of *The Authoritarian Dynamic*

Why Intolerance and Extremism Happen

Understanding Our Deepest Divides

Teri Kanefield

He who knows only his own side
of the case knows little of that.

— John Stuart Mill, *On Liberty*

Table of Contents

OPENING THOUGHTS

In this short book, I tackle some big questions about extremism and what we can do about the anger and division.

To explore these questions, I turned to the work of political psychologists, neuroscientists, professors of political science and journalism, constitutional historians, and more. The groundbreaking work happening across various disciplines offers solid answers to some of the most intriguing questions from legal and political philosophy— questions that, in the past, seemed unanswerable: *Why do people become cruel or allow cruelty to happen? How can we create a better world?* and even: *What is it that makes us human?*

I included a bibliography, but I've also drawn from my own writing. A complete bibliography, therefore, would include the bibliographies from my books *A Firehose of Falsehood: The Story of Disinformation, Free to Be Ruth Bader Ginsburg: The Story of Women and Law,* my Making of America series, and others.

The ancient Greek poet Callimachus is credited with saying, "A big book is a big evil." While I wouldn't go that far, I have found that many nonfiction books are longer and more ponderous than they need to be and stuffed with unnecessary detail.

I have tried to avoid that mistake.

1
Demagogues
and Artists

In September 2024, I went to Chile for the national independence festivities and a family reunion for my husband and his siblings. While there, I learned something that surprised me. One of my in-laws—she's 84 and one of the sweetest people I know—admires Augusto Pinochet. She was firm in her views. I was warned not to talk politics with her, so I didn't. But I talked to others who knew her opinions.

I asked, "Does she know that Pinochet staged a military coup? Does she know he overthrew a legitimately elected president? Does she know he installed himself as a brutal dictator?"

The answer: "Yes, she knows all that. But she says he saved Chile from communism."

This was a woman who worked her entire life as a baker. She never had much money. I struggled to reconcile her economic status and sweet disposition with her support for a brutal dictator.

To make sense of it, I dug deeper into Chilean history.

This is what I learned: Before the troubles began, Chileans prided themselves on having the most stable democracy in South America. Chile also had a high level of income inequality. Then, in 1970, Salvador Allende, co-founder of Chile's Socialist Party, was elected president. After he was inaugurated, he set to work restructuring Chilean society along socialist lines. To address the extreme income inequality, his government authorized large wage increases and froze prices. The government acquired significant privately owned mining and manufacturing assets and took control of large agricultural estates for use by farming cooperatives. Allende's government deducted what it called "excess profits" from compensation owed to US copper companies when nationalizing them.

The Nixon Administration was furious. Foreign investors lost confidence in Chile. The Chilean economy took a dive.

A shortage of basic commodities created a black market. Sporadic violence from the far left continued under Allende, contributing to the polarization and anxiety. People were braced for trouble.

Trouble indeed came. Hardliners opposed to Allende accused him of attempting to "implement totalitarianism in Chile." Allende sought to appease his supporters by pushing harder against his opponents. Chile was in crisis. In the words of Harvard political science professors Steven Levitsky and Daniel Ziblatt, "mutual tolerance disappeared," and instead of compromising, politicians "tried to win at all costs."

Their point is that democracy requires compromise. It requires give and take. It requires people working together. It requires mutual tolerance. When all that mattered was winning, in the words of Ziblatt and Levitsky, "Chileans, who had long prided themselves on being South America's most stable democracy, succumbed to dictatorship."

On September 11, 1973—with US help—Pinochet staged a coup. Tanks rolled into Santiago, and fighter jets bombed the presidential palace. Allende was overthrown.

Pinochet dismantled Allende's reforms, installed himself as dictator, and held power for nearly twenty years. During that time, roughly 28,000 people were arrested for opposing him. Many were tortured or imprisoned. Roughly 3,200 people who opposed him were executed or disappeared.

Pinochet's supporters argued that he responded to a crisis and did what was necessary. They say he was saving the constitution. I could find no credible source that claimed Pinochet followed the law. He was, according to his defenders, using illegal—and brutal—means to save the constitution. In the words of Robert Packenham and historian William Ratliff, writing for the Hoover Institution, Pinochet—who they refer to as a "strongman"—ruled harshly but "left behind the most successful country in Latin America."

Pinochet's power waned in 1988, when he lost a plebiscite. 55 percent voted against extending his rule, while 44 percent still supported him, a reminder that dictators often have real public support.

Today, Chile is a representative, constitutional democracy with a high level of income inequality, which many activists still want to address.

In a 2015 interview, Chilean American poet Marjorie Agosín said, "I think Pinochet has been proven to be an evil dictator in the eyes of most people in the world, and most people see Allende as a dreamer and even a visionary." I had always assumed that was true. But, of course, "most people" does not mean "everyone." Pinochet still has supporters and defenders.

Evil vs. Cruelty

Philosophers have long pondered the meaning and existence of evil. Medieval philosophers steeped in the Christian religion struggled to reconcile the idea of an all-powerful God with the existence of evil. There has also been discussion among philosophers about whether we should even talk about evil. Some claim that evil is nothing more than a word for what we don't understand. Others argue that evil is too often simply a slur against enemies.

I suggest that we use the word *cruel* instead of *evil* because *cruel* doesn't carry the connotation of a grand moral judgment. It has fewer theological implications. It doesn't conjure the idea of supernatural or satanic forces. It's also easier to establish.

Here is the *Oxford American Dictionary* definition of cruelty: "Behavior or actions that deliberately cause pain or distress to people or animals, done either by intention, indifference, or wanton neglect."

Evil requires a particular intention or state of mind, while cruelty doesn't. A small child who tortures an animal is being cruel. Whether the child is evil is a different question, and most likely the answer is no. We must still do some hair-splitting, though, because a doctor setting a broken bone might deliberately inflict pain, but he's not being cruel. On the other hand, criminal punishment is always cruel, but whether it is necessary can be argued.

If we ask whether Pinochet's cruelty was justified, some people will argue yes, and some will argue no. We could say that *evil* means *unjustified cruelty*, which leaves open an argument about whether the cruelty was justified.

Since World War II, there has been renewed interest in the concept of evil as philosophers, psychologists, and others struggled to understand genocides, terrorist acts, and mass killings. One such person was Hannah Arendt, a German-Jewish philosopher and political theorist. She was arrested by the Nazis in 1933 for anti-Nazi activities and, shortly afterward, escaped to France. When the Nazis seized France, they were after her again, so she fled to the United States. In 1961, *The New Yorker* sent her to Jerusalem to cover the trial of Adolf Eichmann, one of the key architects of the Holocaust and an organizer of the death camps.

Eichmann argued at his trial that he had simply been following orders. Arendt was struck by his complete moral indifference and his strict adherence to rules and regulatory order. For Arendt, he represented something more terrifying than an embodiment of Satan or supernatural evil forces. He represented what she called the banality of evil—ordinary people acting from ordinary impulses, such as a desire for promotion or a belief that all rules must be obeyed, who nonetheless participate in actions that bring about mass death.

In Arendt's book *Eichmann in Jerusalem: A Report on the Banality of Evil* that resulted from her reporting of the trial, she rejected the idea that evil is done by people who are depraved or possessed by demonic forces. She argued instead that evil is committed by people who don't think critically and don't consider the moral implications of their actions.

Plato argued that democracy's flaw is that too few people can think deeply about the complex issues inherent in politics. The same flaw obviously applies to other forms of government. Eichmann was not part of a democracy.

A German friend once told me about an experience in the 1990s when he was traveling in the former Soviet Union. Because so many Russians he met experienced the Nazi invasion, he was accustomed to people feeling uncomfortable with him. Then one day a man took him aside and whispered, "I admire what Hitler tried to do." My friend was shocked.

All of this raises the question: How do dictators secure so much support? The answer is that they excel in the art of demagoguery. I'll skip the complicated question about the psyches of dictators and what drives them and simply note that dictators rely on common, highly effective formulas.

And *that* brings us to demagoguery.

The word *democracy* is from ancient Greek. *Demos* means "people," and *cracy* means "to rule." The ancient Greeks also gave us the word *demagogue,* which literally means "a leader of the people," but has come to mean a person, especially a political leader, who seeks support by appealing to popular desires and prejudices rather than by using rational argument. Plato believed that people were too susceptible to the siren call of a demagogue for democracy to be stable.

Demagogues either take advantage of existing chaos or invent a problem and then offer a solution that (1) benefits them and (2) sets them up for the role of savior.

Professor Harold Hill in *The Music Man* offers a striking example of a demagogue at work. Harold Hill tells the citizens of River City this:

> Friend, either you're closing your eyes to a situation
> you do not wish to acknowledge, or you are not aware
> of the caliber of disaster indicated by the presence of a
> pool table in your community. Well, ya got trouble, my
> friend.

(If you want to see a demagogue in action, search for Robert Preston's performance of "Ya Got Trouble" on YouTube.)

Professor Harold Hill—who is not really a professor, he's a con artist—then offers the solution: Buy what he is selling. He follows the classic formula. Frightened people make bad decisions, so scare them. Arouse their fears. When people are frightened enough, they are more likely to follow a demagogue.

Eli Merritt, a political historian at Vanderbilt University, puts the matter more simply. Demagogues destroy democracies, he says. He calls this the "golden rule of democracies." It's the golden rule because democracy—by its very nature—allows for the rise of demagogues. Freedom of speech is required for a demagogue to come to power. At the same time, democracy requires freedom of speech to thrive. People must be free to critique their elected leaders as part of the process of deciding which leaders they want next. If you restrict speech so far that a demagogue cannot possibly arise, you will also remove the same freedom that allows democracy to survive.

See the problem? You can't silence ideas in a democracy, and that includes anti-democratic ideas. The only remedy is for the public to reject demagogues and dangerous ideas.

The Authoritarian Personality

All of this raises a few more questions. First, what makes certain people susceptible to the appeal of a demagogue? Second, is there anything we can do to blunt the power and appeal of a dangerous demagogue while preserving democratic institutions?

As with any interesting set of questions, it wasn't long before scientists sought the answers.

The first researchers were a team at the University of California, Berkeley who investigated this question: "What about human beings allowed for such atrocities as the Nazi death camps?" The team member who became most widely known, Theodor Adorno, was a German sociologist and Marxist who fled Germany in 1934 when the Nazis targeted left-leaning scholars. Because of his background, and because the Nazi atrocities were widely known, the team focused on what we might call right-wing authoritarianism.

The term *authoritarian personality* comes from the title of the book the team published in 1950. The authoritarian personality describes people who fall in line behind an authoritarian leader. The authors used the term *fascist leader* because they were focused on authoritarianism on the right side of the political spectrum. The term *demagogues* is broader and more accurate.

The authors concluded that people with this disposition are, among other things, rigid thinkers who have difficulty with nuance. They have an "intolerance of ambiguity." This adds up to an inability to process complex issues, which is how Arendt described Eichmann. The description of the authoritarian personality also recalls Plato's concern that too many people lack the ability to think about the complex issues involved in politics in order for democracy to work.

True innovators often face harsh criticism. This is partly because new ideas are unsettling, and partly because those who are first cannot have perfected their research methods. Those who are first often don't have the perspective to separate their own biases from their modes of inquiry. The authors of *The Authoritarian Personality* were innovators. Their ideas were unsettling. Their biases—focusing only on extremists on the right side of the political spectrum—were evident. But their book and the answers it suggested spawned an entire field of study that continues to the present.

Political psychologist and behavioral scientist Karen Stenner developed a theory explaining how authoritarian movements arise. She tells us that those with an authoritarian predisposition have a deep need for "oneness and sameness." They want to minimize differences. This can include racial or political differences. Some authoritarians want everyone to abide by the same moral code. Others want everyone to hold the same beliefs. One way or another, people with authoritarian tendencies want sameness. To achieve this, they insist on rules and boundaries, and they seek institutions or authority figures to enforce those boundaries.

Stenner sometimes refers to the authoritarian disposition as "difference-ism." She describes those with this disposition as "avoiders of complexity." Because this disposition is present in about a third of the population across different times and cultures, Stenner refers to being authoritarian as "just another way to be human."

People with this trait often embrace moral absolutism. Some authoritarians may allow political oppression or even seek "punitiveness toward dissidents and deviants."

Stenner stresses that people with this disposition are "malleable and easily exploited." In other words, they easily fall prey to a demagogue or authority figure who arouses their fears.

On the other end of the spectrum are those who are non-authoritarian. They are people who value differences, and the individual freedom that allows for moral and political diversity. Diversity, after all, is a form of complexity. Non-authoritarians are accepting of people who are not like them. They don't expect everyone to think like them or be like them.

Most people fall somewhere between these two extremes.

Stenner's research shows that the authoritarian personality exists on both sides of the political spectrum. A recent study she conducted found that roughly 39 percent of Americans identifying as Republicans are highly authoritarian, compared with about 22 percent of Democrats.

She reminds us that our distinction between "left" and "right" is "not a fundamental and enduring dimension of human nature." A person's designation as "left-wing" or "right-wing" is only weakly correlated to whether that person is predisposed to authoritarianism.

The Political Spectrum

Any political spectrum or chart has limitations. People rarely fit neatly into clear categories. They often hold mixed views. They may shift, depending on the issue. Political movements attract different kinds of people for different reasons. The terms *left* and *right* can mean different things in different countries and eras, and can carry different connotations. Still, labels are a useful shorthand—if we keep their limits in mind.

Traditionally, the political spectrum has been viewed as a line.

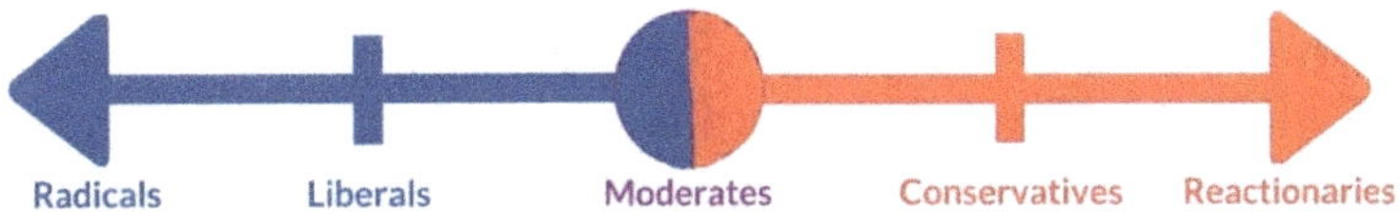

The traditional way of understanding the difference between liberals and conservatives is that conservatives resist change, while liberals seek change. Radicals and reactionaries, in contrast, want rapid change. They want to upset the applecart. What Stenner and psychologist Jonathan Haidt refer to as status quo conservatives try to hold the applecart steady.

Haidt argues that liberals and true conservatives see different threats, push in different directions, and protect different values. They balance each other. He likens this to a yin and yang relationship. As Stenner puts it, "Societies seem to thrive when there's a balanced mix of folks who monitor the boundaries and guard against the strange and unfamiliar, and others who seek out novelty and variety." Without liberals, nothing would improve. Without conservatives, change might move too quickly and become destabilizing. At the same time, liberals and conservatives have trouble understanding each other.

It is often said that the political spectrum is more like a horseshoe.

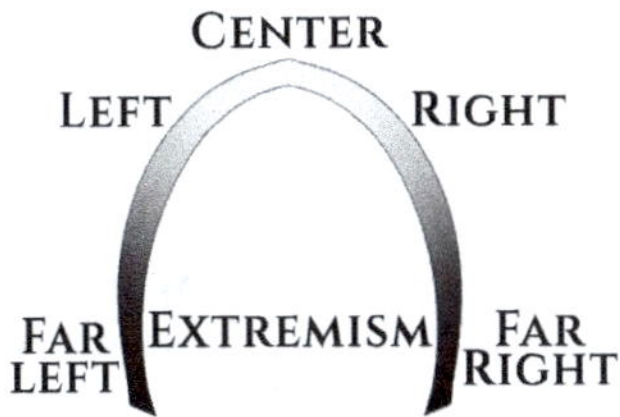

As a person moves toward the ends of the spectrum, they move deeper into extremism. While the two extremes share certain traits, they also diverge in important ways. The reactionaries look backward and pine for a bygone era. Radicals (as the term was traditionally used) look forward to a more perfect tomorrow.

One factor that confuses the terminology is that *liberal* has been used as a slur so often that, in the minds of many, it has lost its original meaning. Another confusing factor is that parties and movements that are not conservative often call themselves conservative. This could be because the party started as conservative and then shifted to the right. It could also be clever marketing on the part of extremist movements.

Conservative suggests a buttoned-down appearance. It feels safe. Similarly, far-left movements sometimes use derogatory labels for liberals who are less extreme.

We are currently witnessing a global surge in right-wing movements. In the United States, we can see this in the rightward shift of the Republican Party.

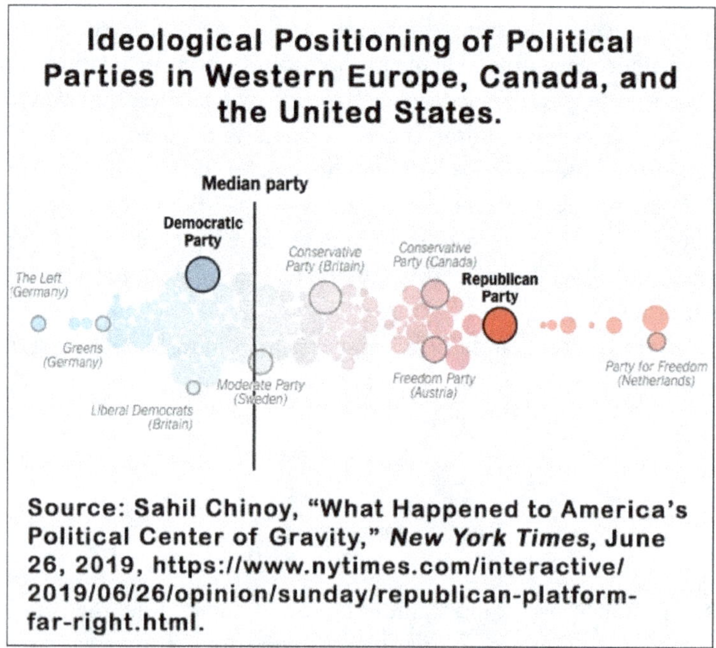

Source: Sahil Chinoy, "What Happened to America's Political Center of Gravity," *New York Times*, June 26, 2019, https://www.nytimes.com/interactive/2019/06/26/opinion/sunday/republican-platform-far-right.html.

A Donald Trump supporter recently smiled at me and said approvingly, "Trump is a radical." Trump wants rapid change. He is upsetting lots of applecarts, and he is doing so in as showy a manner as possible. That is not conservative.

The Authoritarian Dynamic

Stenner and Haidt, in "Authoritarianism Is Not a Momentary Madness, but an Eternal Dynamic Within Liberal Democracies," explain the current rise of right-wing movements worldwide by placing what is happening in the context of what Stenner calls the Authoritarian Dynamic.

The Authoritarian Dynamic works like this:

- Democracy naturally expands and becomes more diverse as out-groups are admitted.

- As democracy expands and becomes more diverse, those with authoritarian dispositions become susceptible to a leader who arouses their fears.

- When the fears of those with authoritarian personalities are aroused, they can become cruel or justify cruelty.

When the fears of those with authoritarian tendencies are not aroused, their authoritarian tendencies will lie dormant. However, when riled by a normative threat—which is something that threatens sameness and order—they can show aggression toward out-groups. They can become cruel and tolerate cruelty in others. Driven by fear, they may be willing to trample rules.

To use the ancient Greek term, the leaders who trigger the fears of authoritarians are demagogues.

As the world becomes more complex and diverse, people with authoritarian personalities recoil. Stenner attributes the current rise of far-right-wing extremist movements worldwide to the simple fact that the complexity of today's world has exceeded many people's capacity to tolerate it. Those who cannot tolerate the cacophony and complexity of today's world become susceptible to leaders who arouse their fears and unleash their authoritarian tendencies.

Can Biology Explain
Our Political Differences?

A study published in *Current Biology* in April 2011, "Political Orientations Are Correlated with Brain Structure in Young Adults," found that people who identify as liberals and people who identify as conservatives show measurable differences in their brains.

MRI scans revealed that self-described conservative students had a larger amygdala than those who identified as liberals. The amygdala is an almond-shaped structure in our brains that becomes active during states of anxiety. The researchers concluded that self-described conservatives are more sensitive to perceived threats, more fearful, and therefore more cautious.

In contrast, students who described themselves as liberal had more gray matter in the anterior cingulate cortex, a region of the brain that helps people cope with complexity.

It makes sense to me that the person who is more cautious and sensitive to threats would prefer the status quo.

The researchers stressed that biology is not destiny. They concluded that a person's political views reflect a combination of genetic influences and environmental factors. Their data, however, suggest a link between brain structure and the psychological mechanisms that lead people to their political inclinations.

It also makes sense to me that the brain can change due to external factors. If you lift weights, the muscles in your arms will change. How much muscle you can build is limited by genetics. Psychologists refer to "thought loops"—repetitive thought patterns that can lead toward cognitive rigidity. As I understand a thought loop, it is like exercising a muscle. Do it often enough and your brain will change in measurable ways.

When I moved from San Francisco to California's central coast in 2017, I hired a contractor to replace a rotted back door to the garage. Once he understood that I had moved from San Francisco, he pegged me as a liberal and tried to goad me into an argument.

It didn't work. He told me that he has guns and likes to sit on his front porch and shoot animals. I offered no response. He mocked Hillary Clinton. I smiled.

I pointed to the door that needed to be replaced—a glass, French-style door—and told him that I wanted another just like it. He said that would be a terrible idea. I asked why. He explained that it would be too easy for someone to break into a glass door. A door to the garage, he said, should be more secure.

I wasn't worried. I said, "I don't have anything in this garage worth stealing."

His response: "A burglar won't know that and will break the glass anyway to search."

I shrugged and said, "Then I'll just leave the door unlocked. That way the burglar won't need to break it."

He stared at me. I assume he was trying to figure out whether I was joking. What I was doing was goading him back. I also wanted a door with windows, and his fears seemed silly to me. Glass doors are a thing. Lots of people have doors with windows.

He was a large man who literally towered over me. I stood firm at my height of 60 inches. "I want a glass door," I said. In fact, I had already selected the one I intended to buy.

I had recently read the article in *Current Biology* and wondered if there was a connection between his fear of burglars and his political views. I also wondered if his need for guns was a result of his fears. At the same time, as a friend later pointed out, I was probably living up to his stereotype of a liberal who was foolish enough to leave doors—and maybe even the borders—unlocked.

As Haidt suggests, maybe a liberal needs someone to remind her to lock the doors because dangers do exist.

Ideological Thinking

Leor Zmigrod, the author of *The Ideological Brain: The Radical Science of Flexible Thinking*, is a political neuroscientist with an impressive resume. When she heard about young British girls drawn to Syria to join ISIS, a question tugged at her: Why were these particular girls lured into extremism? Her book is the result of research into how people spiral into extremism. Among her conclusions is that, given variations in brain structure, some people are more susceptible to the lure of extremism than others.

Her research confirms that biology isn't destiny. She explains how our brains can, through outside influences, become more prone to ideological thinking. She tells us that different people are born with different inclinations toward rigid thinking. Factors such as early indoctrination, fear of death, and panic can make a person more susceptible to ideological thinking. A person's thinking can change over time, becoming more or less flexible depending on environmental factors.

Zmigrod describes ideological thinking as "the style of thinking characterized by rigid adherence to a dogma and a rigid social identity." An ideology, she tells us, is a kind of narrative that tells a compelling story about the world. Not all stories, theories, or ideas are ideologies. An ideology offers an absolutist description of the world and prescribes how we should think, act, and interact with others. Within an ideology, nonconformity is intolerable. Deviation from the rules can lead to severe punishment or ostracism. An ideology demands rigid and ritualistic thinking. People in the grip of an ideology are less curious and less free.

All ideologies, Zmigrod tells us, share particular traits. For example, all ideologies seek a utopia. Stalinists and Leninists looked forward to an ideal world of economic equality. Nazis looked backward to a time when there was perfect order and when they believed the "superior" race ruled.

Any idea or theory can become an ideology if it morphs into a rigid set of rules that grips the brain and essentially turns a person into a fanatic. Zmigrod offers the example of Karl Marx, who advocated freedom from oppression. He hated ideologies, which he believed were used by the ruling class to keep the working class in line. He famously said that religion is the opium of the masses. Then, in the hands of Vladimir Lenin and Joseph Stalin, Marx's philosophy became an ideology used to oppress others.

Zmigrod tells us that when a person is in the grip of an ideology, reverberations of that ideology can be measured in the brain, even when the person is not thinking about politics. In other words, the person's brain actually changes.

Her research showed that those better able to resist ideological thinking have more flexible brains. She measured brain flexibility by observing, through experiments, who was able to switch from one set of rules to another. When the game changes, those with more flexible thinking were able to adapt.

People with inflexible brains tend to be intellectually arrogant. They rarely admit they are wrong. For that matter, they rarely think they are wrong. They don't say, "On the other hand," and see other viewpoints.

People with flexible brains, in contrast, are intellectually humble. They can entertain the possibility that they may be wrong, and they can recognize when they are wrong. Such people are, by nature, freer. In the words of Judge Learned Hand:

> The spirit of liberty is the spirit which is not too
> sure that it is right; the spirit of liberty is the spirit
> which seeks to understand the mind of other men
> and women.

Bertrand Russell illustrated intellectual humility when he quipped, "I would never die for my beliefs because I might be wrong."

Being in the grip of an ideology is satisfying. A complicated world suddenly becomes simple and digestible. Everything makes sense. There are bad guys (our enemies) who are seeking to destroy everything we hold dear. There are good guys (our allies) with whom we stand shoulder-to-shoulder in solidarity.

This is the world:

This is the world with your brain on ideology:

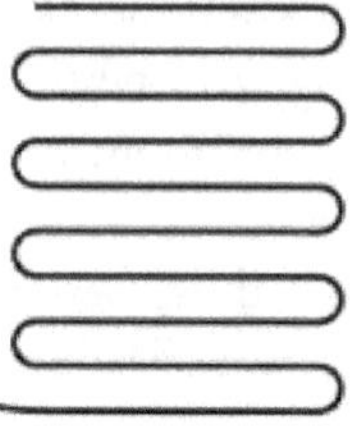

Government, when viewed through an ideological lens, becomes simplified. Forget those complicated civics lessons from your high school government class. If we can just gain control of the government and set things right, we will all live happily ever after in (pick one):

- A perfectly egalitarian democracy.

- A well-ordered society in which all people have personal freedom.

- Some other perfect world.

Here is how Zmigrod describes what happens as a person is drawn into ideological thinking:

> In a given community, everyone will be positioned at different starting points, but the environment they choose (or are forced into) will affect how rapidly the person will adopt the most extreme conclusions of an ideology . . .Once sucked into ideological logic and community, it becomes easier and easier to get drawn more deeply inward—and more difficult to come out.

As the person spirals into ideological thinking, the brain is altered and becomes more accustomed to the ideological thinking. As the brain becomes accustomed to ideological thinking, the spiral becomes tighter and harder to escape. "The spiral," Zmigrod says, "reflects the interaction between a person's dispositions and their ideological environment."

Zmigrod's research led her to conclude that the most flexible thinkers are those just to the left of center on the political spectrum. The least flexible thinkers exist at the extreme points of the political spectrum.

What is striking are the similarities among Zmigrod's descriptions of ideological thinkers, Stenner's description of those with authoritarian personalities, and the study in *Current Biology* showing brain differences associated with different political leanings. Stenner and Zmigrod both describe rigid thinkers as people who insist on conformity, people who prefer absolutes, and people who are less open-minded. The study in *Current Biology* confirms that political differences are measurable in the brain.

When different researchers in different fields using different methods of inquiry come to the same conclusions, there is less chance that the conclusions are the result of bias or a flaw in their research methods. In other words, we can conclude that there is something going on with this whole brain-structure-and-politics thing.

Ideologies Soothe
Existence Pain

Existence pain, as you might expect, is the pain that comes from merely existing as a human. Existence pain includes our awareness of our mortality. It involves confronting what can feel like the meaninglessness of life. It means fearing the loss of those we love. If we don't have loved ones, it means facing solitude. It means fearing the isolation that often accompanies old age. Existence pain includes grappling with the indifference of the universe. It means knowing that what lies ahead—should we live long enough—is physical pain as our bodies break down. It means facing the possibility that there may not be a grand eternal plan.

In the words of psychiatrist Irvin D. Yalom, existence pain is the "pain that is always there, whirring continuously just beneath the membrane of life." It is knowing that "our deepest wants can never be fulfilled ... a halt to aging, the return of vanished ones, eternal love, significance, immortality itself."

The First Noble Truth in Buddhist philosophy emphasizes that life is full of suffering. "Existence pain" is another way of saying the same thing.

Ideologies offer relief from existence pain. An ideology may offer the promise of an afterlife. It may give life a purpose. It may offer the promise of a grand eternal plan. It may offer camaraderie. It soothes the pain of existence and gives meaning to our suffering.

To echo the ideas of Friedrich Nietzsche, people spend their lives searching for the purpose of life as though it must be something beyond itself. But the purpose of a lion's life is to be a lion. This suggests that the purpose of a human's life is simply to be a human. As I understand that, the purpose of our lives is to strive to become more fully human. That requires us to develop our most unique capacities: the rational and socially oriented thinking enabled by our advanced brain regions.

If, as Aristotle famously said, "man is a rational animal," the purpose of our lives should be to become more rational.

And how do we do that?

One way is to turn to the artists. Almost all the arts use metaphor or symbol to some degree. Robert Sapolsky, a neuroscientist and primatologist at Stanford University, tells us that among the qualities that are uniquely human is the ability to think in metaphor and symbols. So, when we practice using metaphors, we are using a part of the brain that is uniquely human.

The visual artist teaches us to see both beauty and pain. In an essay called "The Decay of Lying," Oscar Wilde rejects the widely held idea that art imitates life. Instead, he suggests that life imitates art. He goes even further and argues that nature itself takes its cues from art.

You might say that the nineteenth-century landscape painter Joseph Mallord William Turner taught us to see the beauty in sunsets.

The Fighting Temeraire Tugged to Her Last Berth to Be Broken Up,
by Joseph Mallord William Turner (1838)

Wilde says no. He says that the beauty in landscapes exists *because* the artist taught us how to see it. Nature, he says, literally follows the landscape painter and takes her effects from the artist.

Wilde explained it like this:

> Where, if not from the Impressionists, do we get those wonderful brown fogs that come creeping down our streets, blurring the gas lamps and changing the houses into monstrous shadows? To whom, if not their master, do we owe the lovely silver mists that brood over our river . . .
>
> For what is Nature? Nature is no great mother who has borne us. She is our creation. It is in our brain that she quickens to life. Things are because we see them, and what we see, and how we see it, depends on the Arts that have influenced us . . .
>
> At present, people see fogs, not because there are fogs, but because poets and painters have taught them the mysterious loveliness of such effects. There may have been fogs for centuries in London. I dare say there were. But no one saw them, and so we do not know anything about them. They did not exist till Art had invented them.
>
> Yesterday evening Mrs. Arundel insisted on my going to the window, and looking at the glorious sky, as she called it. Of course I had to look at it. And what was it? It was simply a very second-rate Turner, a Turner of a bad period, with all the painter's worst faults exaggerated and over-emphasized.

Of course, fogs and sunsets exist without a viewer, but what we see as beautiful is shaped by experience, learning, and cultural expectations. Wilde's argument is that, because what we consider to be nature and what we consider to be beautiful are our own constructions, and because the artist teaches us to see beauty, nature does indeed take her effects from the artist.

In the 1980s, I attended a lecture at the Massachusetts Institute of Technology. The lecturer, a historian, marveled at the fact that a group of medieval monks traveling through the Alps never once commented on—or even seemed to see—the glorious beauty of the landscape. Well, of course they didn't see it. That was before the Romantic era landscape painters taught people to see the beauty in a wild and rugged landscape. Very likely, the monks saw only a dangerous, difficult-to-travel wilderness in which they might at any moment be attacked by animals. They were not wrong. It *was* a dangerous wilderness. Nobody had taught them to also see the beauty.

Samuel Coleridge famously said, "I have a smack of Hamlet myself." It's possible that many of us have a little Hamlet in us, which means Shakespeare taught us to see something in ourselves.

If we imitate literary figures and then, through the imitation, absorb some of those characteristics, isn't life imitating art? The little girl obsessed with Disney princesses who wears her princess outfit and practices being special learns the lesson Sara Crewe learned in Frances Hodgson Burnett's *The Little Princess*: "I am a princess. All girls are!"

Life imitates art.

A classical tragedy can show how well-meaning human beings, through their actions or inactions, can create unnecessary pain and suffering. In other words, a classical tragedy can explore how people become cruel.

Antigone by the ancient Greek playwright Sophocles does exactly that. Here is the plot in a nutshell. Creon, the king, makes a law that Antigone, a citizen, knows is unjust. Antigone disobeys the law because she would rather be a good person than a good citizen. Creon is determined to punish her because he insists that all order and civilization will break down if citizens don't obey the law. In his zeal to punish Antigone, Creon becomes vengeful and cruel. In the end, he destroys himself and those he loves.

The German philosopher Georg Wilhelm Friedrich Hegel, in his *Lectures on Aesthetics,* said that *Antigone* was "one of the most sublime and in every respect the most excellent work of art of all time." He believed the play was about opposing moral claims: Creon claims that justice requires punishing all people who break the law. Antigone claims that justice means doing what is right.

Antigone teaches us that important questions about power, government, law, and punishment defy easy answers. After absorbing *Antigone,* we can see what is wrong with the law-and-order people who shake their fists and shout, "All lawbreakers must be punished, or the rule of law will be destroyed!"

The artist helps us confront and process the complexity of life.

Art can also show us we are not alone in our emotions. Among the most iconic of all paintings, *The Scream* (1893) by Edvard Munch, captures nothing less than the cacophony, uncertainty, and anxiety of the modern age.

While wandering through an art gallery, I was struck by the work of French painter Stéphanie Ledroit. With her permission, I am including some of her artwork here.

We are essentially social creatures, so we naturally fear isolation. The phrase "In the end we are all alone," which has been attributed to various sources, therefore resonates.

Ledroit shows us that solitude can be a time of renewal, a time to look inward, a time of creativity, or a time to discover new things about ourselves. She uncovers the beauty that can be found in isolation. I asked her why she often paints children, and she said, "Because they naturally slip into their own space."

The Artist and the Demagogue

The demagogue riles us to hate and fear and makes us more brutal, more simplistic, less human, and less humane. Conversely, the true artist teaches us to embrace complexity and become more fully human.

Before law school when I taught college English, I always ended my lessons on metaphors and similes by writing on the board, "Metaphors Be with You." At the time, I thought I was offering a joke. In fact, I was offering sage advice for how to cultivate a habit of mind that grows accustomed to complexity and can withstand easy answers. I was also offering advice for how to become more fully human.

The more we practice embracing complexity—and the more we work on expanding our sympathies, however we choose to do it, like a gymnast stretching her muscles—the more flexible our thinking can become, and the better we are able to withstand ideological thinking.

That, I believe, is what Fyodor Dostoevsky meant when he said, "The world will be saved by beauty."

2
"These Are the Times
That Try Men's Souls"

The phrase, "These are the times that try men's souls" is the opening line from the first pamphlet in a series written by Thomas Paine and published in December of 1776.

When the pamphlet was published, the Continental Army had just been defeated. Enlistments were running out. Paine's pamphlet was a rallying cry intended to persuade and encourage the colonists to keep fighting the war.

In 1967, political scientist Murray Edelman said, "All times are 'the times that try men's souls.' The age one lives in is always in crisis, and especially so since newspaper reading became common."

According to Edelman, newspaper reading changed everything because suddenly people were informed of events outside their immediate experience. Edelman argues that because most political events are outside the immediate experience of most citizens, almost all political events are presented by means of symbols or abstractions.

To illustrate Edelman's idea, let's take the example of the dwindling interest in the Revolutionary War at the end of 1776. Most Americans at the time were subsistence farmers or laborers. Historian John Ferling, author of *A Leap in the Dark*, tells us that one of the main drivers in the Revolutionary War was the heavy-handed manner that the British exerted control over the colonies, including finding ways to extract money from the colonists. In other words, colonists didn't like being taxed by a faraway government, which is why the Tea Party was a defining moment.

Much of the Continental Army's rank and file soldiers were landless laborers and men from the lower social strata who were drawn to enlist by bounties, pay, or land promises, but it also included a significant number of subsistence farmers. We can assume, therefore, that the price of tea did not affect their daily lives. Moreover, the colonists were not simply fighting against a faraway king. They were challenging the dominant global superpower of the eighteenth century, which meant there was a good chance they would be killed. Subsistence farmers probably didn't want to leave the fields that fed their families and risk their lives in a war just so someone they voted for would have a say in their tax bills, particularly if there was no guarantee that their taxes would go down.

The farmer needed a reason worth dying for, and those reasons were given as abstractions like *Independence!* and *Liberty!*

Edelman explains that "all times are the times that try men's souls" because every political act terrifies someone while reassuring someone else. The McCarthy period of anti-communist campaigns in the early 1950s was terrifying to those who saw the government seeking out and punishing people for their political views as an abhorrent violation of civil liberties and the First Amendment. On the other hand, it was reassuring to those who were terrified of a Stalinist-style communist revolution and believed that aggressive action was necessary to prevent the spread of communism. They saw what happened in Russia after the Russian Revolution, and they were afraid the same thing would happen in the United States.

To some, the McCarthy era was the worst of times. To others, McCarthy's supporters, it was the best of times because someone was aggressively rooting out the danger of communism.

Let's take, as another example, the campus protests of the 1960s when protest movements broke out on high school and college campuses across the United States. Student activists demanded, among other things, civil rights for all Americans, women's rights, and an end to the United States military involvement in Vietnam. They wanted to abolish ROTC programs on college campuses, and they protested police brutality. Protesters organized sit-ins and strikes.

The protests were terrifying to those who viewed them as chaotic, lawless, and endangering what had been the American way of life for centuries. For such people, everything was topsy-turvy. White students marched with Black students. Women wore pants. Men grew their hair long. The birth control pill threatened to disrupt what people thought of as the stability of the American family. Young people were experimenting with drugs. The music was different and unsettling.

For others, the protests of the 1960s were part of a thrilling and liberating period of about twenty-six years that witnessed the end of legalized racial segregation and the signing of the Civil Rights Act of 1964, the Voting Rights Act of 1965, and the Immigration Act of 1965.

Let's pause for a moment to reflect on the Immigration and Nationality Act of 1965 and the long-term effects, because it is creating some of the division we see today. The Act, among other things, abolished national-origin quota systems, which had previously favored white immigrants. As a result, over the coming decades, there was a profound shift in the nation's demographics because of increased immigration from Asia, Latin America, and Africa.

What that means is these pieces of legislation, the Civil Rights Act, the Voting Rights Act, and the Immigration Act, transformed America from mostly white to a more multicultural nation.

That twenty-six-year period from the Supreme Court's 1954 decision in *Brown v. Board of Education*—the case that ended legalized racial segregation—until the election of Ronald Reagan was a time of rapid change that some found exhilarating and others found terrifying. It was the best of times, it was the worst of times, but not because good and bad existed together. It was the best of times and the worst of times because for some, it was the best of times. For others, it was the most unsettling of times.

The Founding Conditions

Recall that regressives, or far-right extremists, pine for a bygone era. To understand regressives in a democratic government, we have to understand what Hungarian political scientist and former Minister of Human Capacities of Hungary Bálint Magyar called the founding conditions and the Democratic Big Bang, the event or series of events that established a democratic government. Magyar says that the founding conditions preceding the Democratic Big Bang have a decisive role in the formation of the system.

The American Democratic Big Bang is, of course, the Revolutionary War and the ratification of the U.S. Constitution. The Russian Democratic Big Bang, in contrast, occurred in the early 1990s when the former Soviet Union broke up. Preceding the Russian Democratic Big Bang was a communist dictatorship in which the Communist Party controlled everything, including all the nation's industries and resources. After the Democratic Big Bang, when the Russians tried to create a democracy but before democracy was firmly established, the people we now call the ruling oligarchs seized the nation's resources and control of the central government. By 2012, Russia was once more a dictatorship.

In other words, within a few decades, Russian regressives pushed the nation all the way back to the founding conditions. Masha Gessen, in *The Future is History: How Totalitarianism Reclaimed Russia,* argues that this was possible because, during the lengthy period of Soviet dictatorship, Russians developed habits and psychological states that conditioned them to authoritarianism. The founding conditions set the baseline.

In contrast to the Russian founding conditions, here are the conditions that preceded the American Democratic Big Bang:

- The colonies that formed the United States had functioning democratic institutions such as jury trials, local elected governments that managed the day-to-day business of the colonies, and constitutions that protected the rights of the colonists. The hitch was that the democratic institutions protected only the rights of white men, but there *were* democratic institutions with a long history. The *Zenger* trial illustrates how deeply freedom of the press was entrenched in the founding conditions.

- There was a strict social hierarchy with white men at the top and Black women at the bottom. Slavery was part of that hierarchy. The assumption was later articulated by James Henry Hammond, a South Carolina Senator and wealthy enslaver, who said that every society has a hierarchy, and those at the bottom serve as "mudsills" to create the foundation or support. In other words, those at the bottom of the hierarchy labor for the benefit of those at the top.

- Women who were not enslaved had minimal rights.

- Most American colonists and early Americans were Protestant.

- The nation was almost entirely rural. According to the Census Bureau, the percentage of the US population in 1790 living in a city of 2,500 or more was 5.1 percent. At the time of the Revolutionary War, less than 4 percent of colonists lived in cities.

- Most power resided locally. The result was that there were very few restrictions on what white men could do.

- Gun ownership was part of everyday life for white men in colonial and early America. This was particularly true where there were fears of attacks by Native Americans or uprisings among the enslaved population. Gun laws restricted the rights of non-whites to carry guns. The colonists and early Americans didn't want the Native Americans or those enslaved getting their hands on guns. Some areas had laws mandating that white men carry guns.

In other words, the founding conditions were that white men ruled a mostly rural nation that was almost entirely governed locally with very few restrictions on white men.

It was the best of times, it was the worst of times—depending on who you were. Thomas Jefferson had it pretty good.

Now compare the conditions today.

- Our Constitution states in the Fourteenth Amendment that democratic institutions protect all people equally.

- Women have the full rights of citizenship and are in positions of leadership.

- The nation is no longer rural. As of 2022, approximately 80 percent of Americans lived in areas considered urban, which is now defined as a city with more than 5,000 people.

- Protestants are no longer the majority. As of 2024, only 40 percent of Americans described themselves as Protestant.

- In 2024, white voters made up 71% of the electorate. This is down from 95% during the 1950s. The percentage of white voters has been steadily dropping.

- We have gun control laws (well, a few).

The thing to remember about these changes is that almost all of them happened since the 1950s. That means there are Americans alive today who remember a nation ruled by white Protestant men.

When the most extreme American regressives want to take us back to a bygone era, the conditions they yearn for are those that preceded and immediately followed the Democratic Big Bang. Consider this definition of Christian nationalism, as described in *Christianity Today*:

> Christian nationalism is the belief that the American nation is defined by Christianity, and that the government should take active steps to keep it that way.

> America is defined by its 'Anglo-Protestant' past, and
> we will lose our identity and our freedom if we do not
> preserve our cultural identity.

Anglo, of course, means white. Notice the use of the words "freedom" and "we."

When the Bill of Rights was drafted, at least six states had government-supported churches. The state governments of each of the thirteen states promoted the religion of their choice. Eleven of the thirteen states had religious qualifications for holding an office. South Carolina, for example, had a provision in its constitution about religion. The first sentence of the provision says this:

> All persons and religious societies who acknowledge
> that there is one God, and a future state of rewards and
> punishments, and that God is publicly to be worshiped,
> shall be freely tolerated.

In other words, you will not be tolerated if you don't agree that God is to be publicly worshiped. The next sentences say this:

> The Christian Protestant religion shall be deemed,
> and is hereby constituted and declared to be, the
> established religion of this state. That all denominations
> of Christian Protestants in this State, demeaning
> themselves peaceably and faithfully, shall enjoy equal
> religious and civil privileges.

So, the founding conditions included a requirement that people worship in the approved manner.

The First Amendment opens with the Establishment Clause:

> Congress shall make no law respecting an establishment
> of religion, or prohibiting the free exercise thereof.

It was understood in 1791, when the Bill of Rights was ratified, that "Congress shall make no law" referred to the US Congress. The Establishment Clause stated that the federal government did not have the power to impose a religion on the nation. State governments, however, could do as they wished. It wasn't until the mid-twentieth century that the United States Supreme Court held that the Establishment Clause applied to the states as well as the federal government. The decision was controversial and stirred a considerable amount of anger among some Christian groups.

When Supreme Court Justice Clarence Thomas wrote in 2004 that the Establishment Clause was not intended to protect individual rights, it was intended to protect states' rights, he was not wrong. The counterargument is that a lot has changed in 200 years—including the Fourteenth Amendment that was ratified after the Civil War and requires states to respect the rights of individuals. Moreover, a great many Americans simply do not want to live in the eighteenth century.

The regressive view of American history is that something vital is being lost or destroyed. Regressives see history as a gradual downward slope, something that started off good and pure and has been sliding downhill.

The progressive view, in contrast, is that American history has been a gradual upward slope. The progressive view is that the Founders had some pretty good ideas: The idea of a government based on rule of law instead of the whim of a king, the idea of an independent judiciary, and a government that represents "we the people." The problem, for progressives, is that the Founders left out a lot of people. Most progressive forward pushes in American history have been attempts to include more people.

Here's the catch: Each push forward triggered a backlash. The more dramatic the changes, the stronger the backlash. Progressives who expect the upward slope to continue, or conservatives who expect things to remain the same, can experience extreme shock when that does not happen.

Race and the Law

Now let's look at how, in the United States, the reactionary desire to return to the founding conditions comes into constant conflict with a progressive yearning for a better tomorrow. The place to start is with the history of race and the law.

At the start of the Civil War, the South removed its representatives from Congress because they intended to leave the Union. When the war ended, Congress refused to readmit the former Confederates until they agreed to a few conditions. Among the conditions was that the former Confederate states must ratify the Thirteenth, Fourteenth, and Fifteenth Amendments—the Amendments known as the Civil War Amendments or Reconstruction Amendments. The Thirteenth Amendment ended slavery or involuntary servitude "except as a punishment for a crime whereof the party shall have been duly convicted." The Fourteenth Amendment guaranteed (among other things) equal protection and equal rights for all people. The Fifteenth Amendment removed race as a barrier to voting.

The important point here is that the former Confederates did not agree willingly to these Amendments. The Amendments were literally forced on them.

For a brief time after the Civil War before the South regrouped and regained power, Black Americans enjoyed civil rights. Black men were even elected to local offices. Then came the massive pushback, culminating in 1896, when the United States Supreme Court, which was largely sympathetic to the former Confederacy, ruled that racial segregation was legal under the Fourteenth Amendment.

That ushered in the era of legalized racial segregation and widespread voter suppression. The goal was to keep white men in control.

Former Confederates also found ways to exploit the exception in the Thirteenth Amendment that allows forced servitude if the person was convicted in court. Law enforcement at the time was local with minimal constitutional restrictions, so Black men were charged with crimes and convicted on scant or nonexistent evidence by all-white juries. Sometimes the police, after arresting a Black man, would beat a confession out of him. Other times they bypassed the judicial process altogether, and the Black person was lynched. Those who were convicted were put into chain gangs and forced to work.

Then, in the 1930s, Thurgood Marshall, Charles Hamilton Houston, and their team of lawyers organized and spent decades formulating and carrying out a legal strategy to end legalized racial segregation, protect voting rights, and secure rights for people accused of crimes. Their many achievements included the following:

- *Chambers v. Florida* (1940) addressed the problem of police officers beating confessions out of defendants.

- *Smith v. Allwright* (1944) secured important voting rights for Black Americans.

- *Brown v. Board of Education* (1954) ended legalized racial segregation in the United States.

These decisions, particularly *Brown v. Board of Education*, paved the way for the modern Civil Rights Movement, which in turn made possible the modern women's movement.

So, for 200 years, change was gradual. In the 1950s, racial segregation was still legal. There were places in the United States where Black Americans were entirely cut off from white America. Job discrimination meant that Black Americans were mostly confined to menial labor. Housing options were limited due to widespread discriminatory practices. Segregated schools meant that Black children often received an inferior education.

Then, over a period of about twenty-five years beginning with the U.S. Supreme Court's decision in *Brown v. Board of Education*, rapid changes created new opportunities for people who had previously been denied many of the rights and privileges of citizenship.

The face of America was changing.

*Changing Laws Governing
Women's Dependence on Men*

Understanding how the founding conditions regarding women have changed is essential for understanding the goal of some of today's extremist movements.

At the time the United States was founded, there was a legal doctrine known as the doctrine of coverture. Under this doctrine, a woman had no legal identity apart from her husband. That meant, among other things, that a married woman could not be sued, could not enter into contracts, could not borrow money, and could not own property in her own name.

Then, after the Civil War, came the Fourteenth Amendment, which said, "nor shall any state ... deny to any person within its jurisdiction the equal protection of the laws."

Women read the Fourteenth Amendment, saw the words *any person* and thought they should be included.

One such woman was Myra Colby Bradwell, who was born in 1831. She wanted to be a lawyer, and submitted her application for a law license as required by law in Illinois. Her application contained the required court certificate attesting to her good character and the results of her examination, showing that she was qualified to practice law.

The Illinois Supreme Court denied her request for a law license because her status as a married woman would prevent her from practicing law. How, for example, could she sign legal agreements with her clients if she needed her husband's permission each time she wanted to enter into a contract?

Bradwell challenged the decision. The Illinois Supreme Court issued its final response, relying on the fallback position that the Illinois legislature did not intend women to practice law, so the court had no authority to grant a law license to a woman.

Bradwell brought her case to the U.S. Supreme Court. Her argument was a simple one. The Fourteenth Amendment plainly decreed that no state may deny any person equal protection of the laws. She was a person. The Illinois law deprived her of equal protection by refusing to allow her to practice law on the basis of her gender. Therefore, the Illinois law violated the Constitution, and she must be permitted a law license.

The United States Supreme Court ruled against her, saying, "That God designed the sexes to occupy different spheres of action, and that it belonged to men to make, apply, and execute the laws, was regarded as an almost axiomatic truth." This is from Justice Bradley's widely quoted concurrence:

> Man is, or should be, woman's protector and defender. The natural and proper timidity and delicacy that belongs to the female sex evidently unfits it for many of the occupations of civil life. The Constitution of the family organization, which is founded in the divine ordinance as well as in the nature of things, indicates the domestic sphere as that which properly belongs to the domain and functions of womanhood. The harmony, not to say identity, of interest and views which belong, or should belong, to the family institution is repugnant to the idea of a woman adopting a distinct and independent career from that of her husband.

Justice Bradley concluded:

> The paramount destiny and mission of a woman is to fulfill the noble and benign offices of wife and mother. This is the law of the Creator. And the rules of civil society must be adapted to the general constitution of things, and cannot be based upon exceptional cases.

Because women were prevented from entering most professions and had limited means of earning a living, most women had to get married. Because divorce was almost impossible to obtain, and wife-beating was generally not considered a crime (see, for example, *State v. A. B. Rhodes*, 1886), women were effectively trapped. To borrow Susan B. Anthony's words, "Woman's sustenance is in the hands of men, and arbitrarily and unjustly he exercises his power over her."

In her attempt to bring about equal rights for women, Anthony knocked on doors and tried to talk to women about their rights. Many told her they had all the rights they wanted. Some said they didn't want equal rights and slammed doors in her face. In her words, she'd "embarked on an unpopular case and must be content to row upstream." How did she keep going? She told herself she was working, not for her contemporaries, many of whom would never appreciate her work, but for "future generations we must labor."

For 200 years, change was slow and there were setbacks. Women in the 1950s, for example, had fewer job opportunities than women in the 1940s because, with so many men off fighting World War II, women were needed to keep the economy moving. When the men returned from the war, women were expected to return to the home. The 1950s, therefore, were more repressive than the 1940s.

Before the Civil Rights Act of 1964, women could be discriminated against in the job market based on their gender.

Before 1974, banks and credit card companies could—and often did—refuse credit cards to women, especially married women, unless they had a male co-signer. Then, in 1974, President Gerald Ford signed into law the Equal Credit Opportunity Act that prohibited banks and credit card companies from discriminating against applicants based on gender or marital status. Even then, discrimination continued due to loopholes.

Thus, from the nation's founding until the mid-twentieth century, not much changed for women. They had to marry. They had trouble finding employment because they were expected to be housewives. Before the birth control pill was widely available, the only real option for most women was to marry and have children.

Then, over the past seventy years, everything changed. Women now can freely enter the workforce and hold positions of power. They can take out loans, borrow money, and buy their own houses. They can say no to marriage and children.

Laws Governing Rape

The history of rape laws helps us understand the rise of such movements as the incels.

Throughout most of Western history, rape was a property crime. An unmarried woman was her father's property. A married woman was her husband's property. If a virgin was raped, the property damage was to her father. If she was married, the damage was to her husband. If she wasn't a virgin and wasn't married, there was no crime because the property was already damaged. A man couldn't rape his wife, his own property, and the rape of enslaved women wasn't a crime. Attempted rape wasn't a crime because there was no property damage.

Rape laws were generally intended to protect (white) men from false accusations. They were not intended to protect a woman from attack.

The social hierarchy determined how rape was treated. Black men were often convicted or lynched if accused of rape by a white woman. White men were protected from rape prosecutions because, until the end of the nineteenth century and into the twentieth century, women were often not considered competent to testify in court. If the only witness to the crime was the victim, and the victim was a woman, and the accused was a white man, it could be difficult to find admissible evidence. Obviously, given the nature of the crime, the woman and the perpetrator were often the only people present.

Rape was seen as the natural result of human nature: Men were viewed as natural aggressors ("boys will be boys"). Because rape was seen as human nature, a woman was responsible for guarding the goods. If she was raped, it meant she failed. Her behavior was therefore taken into account. How was she dressed? Was she out alone? Did she scream or call for help? Did she put up enough resistance—even though most women cannot overpower a male attacker, and generally not without sustaining other injuries.

Susan Brownmiller, in her book *Against Our Will: Men, Women, and Rape*, sent shock waves when she argued that rape was not a natural result of human nature. She said that rape is the means by which all men keep all women in fear. She made the startling claim that rape is a means of exerting patriarchal power. She said that all men, even those who would never rape a woman, benefit from the fact that there are rapists because the fear of rapists means that women need male protection.

As late as the 1970s, a defendant in a rape trial could present evidence that the woman had engaged in sexual behavior in the past. This was called the "sexual history" defense, and was based on these assumptions:

- She previously failed to guard the goods.

- The goods were already "damaged."

- She was unchaste or immoral, which meant her word could not be trusted.

It wasn't until the 1970s and 1980s, under pressure from women's activists, that states enacted what are called "rape shield laws." These laws protect victims and prevent their sexual history from being used as a defense. Nonetheless, the "unchaste victim" exception, which was based on the idea that if the woman was unchaste, the rape did no "damage," survived in some states into the 1990s. Mississippi was the last state to remove the unchaste victim exception in 1998.

As with the laws governing racial relations, for most of our history, things didn't change much. Then, from the 1960s until now, women have steadily gained rights and autonomy.

The Supreme Court
Slowed Things Down

One reason progress was slow for 200 years in the United States is that, for most of our history, we have had a conservative Supreme Court. Then, for a brief period beginning in the 1950s, we had a liberal Supreme Court.

For most of our history, the Supreme Court has been extremely conservative, perhaps even reactionary. Consider *Dred Scott v. Sanford* (1857). The majority held that "a Negro, whose ancestors were imported and sold as slaves," whether enslaved or free, could not be an American citizen and therefore did not have standing to sue in federal court. In addition, the Court held that "the special rights and immunities guaranteed to citizens do not apply to them." The Court also added that enslaved persons were property under the Fifth Amendment and that any law that would deprive a slave owner of that property was unconstitutional.

It took a Civil War to undo that one.

In 1883, the Supreme Court effectively overturned the Civil Rights Act of 1875 that prohibited racial discrimination in public accommodations such as hotels, restaurants, and transportation. The Supreme Court in an 8-1 decision, held that Congress could not regulate private businesses.

In *Plessy v. Ferguson* (1896), the Supreme Court held that separate facilities do not violate the Fourteenth Amendment, thereby legalizing segregation on public transportation.

In *Lochner v. New York* (1905), the Supreme Court said that a law limiting bakery work to ten hours per day was unconstitutional. The Court found an implied liberty of contract in the Due Process Clause. In other words, the Court held that under the freedom to enter contracts, if people were willing to work for a few pennies per day, the government had no authority to step in.

There was also the time the Supreme Court said that the federal income tax was unconstitutional. We needed a constitutional amendment to undo that one. And there was the time the Supreme Court upheld the internment of Japanese Americans during World War II, and the time the Supreme Court held that Georgia had the right to criminalize sexually active gay and lesbian relationships.

The list goes on.

There have been a few exceptions, most notably the Warren Court of the 1950s and the 1960s that gave us such cases as *Brown v. Board of Education*. The early Burger Court gave us *Roe v. Wade,* where the Court found that the Constitution included an implied right to privacy, and that right included the right to an abortion (with exceptions). The backlash from *Roe v. Wade* was fierce, and, because the religious right was galvanized to action, it helped elect Ronald Reagan in 1980.

Before taking her place on the Supreme Court, Ruth Bader Ginsburg spent her career as an activist lawyer working to change the law to help women gain autonomy. Ginsburg, who wasn't yet on the Court when *Roe v. Wade* was decided, agreed with the conclusion. However, she was highly critical of the Court's reasoning. She said the Court should have decided the case under the Equal Protection Clause of the Fourteenth Amendment instead of the idea that the Constitution contains an implied right to privacy. The first rule of statutory interpretation is that you cannot add words that are not there. She also believed the decision was broader than it needed to be. Across the nation, states were changing their laws to make abortion more accessible. She believed the trend would continue.

Ginsburg was an incrementalist who believed that change is better in small increments to allow people a chance to adjust. As an incrementalist, she also believed that Supreme Court decisions should go no farther than necessary to adjudicate the issues before it. She worried that *Roe v. Wade* was too abrupt and sweeping. She accurately predicted that the sweeping nature of the ruling would create a powerful backlash.

The chief complaint of social conservatives is that the ruling in *Roe v. Wade* rests on a precarious constitutional argument. They accused the Supreme Court of making law instead of interpreting the law. They similarly argued that the Constitution says nothing at all about abortion or privacy rights, so how can the Constitution protect those rights?

The Rise of the Incel Movement

For women who enjoy bodily autonomy, the women's movement ushered in the best of times. For a group that calls itself incels, it was the worst of times.

Incels began as a benign online community in 1997 for people who had difficulty forming romantic relationships. The term *involuntary celibate* was first abbreviated to *invcel* and then *incel.*

The founder of the website went by the name Alana. After a few years, she became comfortable with her own bisexuality and gave up control of the website. Over the next fourteen years, the users radicalized into a group of vocal and angry men who resented the fact that women can—and often do—say no.

Today, *incel* describes men who seek to undo gender equality. They complain loudly about their frustration that women are not available to them. Many members advocate coercion and rape.

A 2022 study, "Involuntary Celibacy: A Review of Incel Ideology and Experiences with Dating, Rejection, and Associated Mental Health and Emotional Sequelae," published in *Current Psychiatry Reports,* outlines some ideologies that tie incel communities together. Among other things, incels believe that women are too sexually selective and use their privilege (they get to decide) for social advancement.

Changes will always feel to some people like something vital has been lost. In a sense, men *have* lost something. It was the prerogative, for example, of a wealthy man to have access to beautiful women. That was what Trump was alluding to in the famous *Access Hollywood* tape when he said the following:

> Yeah, that's her with the gold. I better use some Tic Tacs just in case I start kissing her. You know I'm automatically attracted to beautiful...I just start kissing them. It's like a magnet. Just kiss. I don't even wait. And when you're a star they let you do it. You can do anything.

When the recording became public shortly before the 2016 presidential election, many people expected it to derail Trump's campaign. Just over a month later, Trump won the election. I suspect that enough people, both men and women, saw nothing wrong with what Trump said. The incels were probably cheering.

And now, for an amusing aside. When I taught college English, I received a memorable course evaluation from an angry student. The student accused me of "ruining a perfectly innocent fairy tale" because I told the class that *Little Red Riding Hood* is a rape allegory. I said the story is a warning to girls not to wander off into the woods alone because they might not be lucky enough to be rescued by a good huntsman. I explained that the story is a warning to girls about how they should behave and a reminder that they need a male protector.

The student evidently thought I was just a dirty-minded English instructor, but I stand by the rape-allegory interpretation. I mean, for goodness' sake, when the big bad wolf attacks Red Riding Hood, he's in Grandma's *bed*. The wolf is obviously a metaphorical wolf and not a real wolf because a real wolf can't say, "The better to see you with, my dear." And tell me again the color of the girl's hood.

Listen to Sam the Sham sing "Little Red Riding Hood," and I think you'll see that Sam the Sham agreed with me. His song includes lyrics such as these:

> Hey there, Little Red Riding Hood,
> You sure are lookin' good,
> You're everything a big, bad wolf could want.

Sam the Sham's recording is available on YouTube. If *Little Red Riding Hood* was a perfectly innocent fairy tale, I wasn't the first to ruin it.

Originalism and the Rise of the Modern Militia Movement

In response to the liberal Supreme Court of the 1950s, 1960s, and 1970s and the resulting changes, a new constitutional interpretation emerged called originalism. Originalism holds that a law or legal text should be interpreted as it was intended by the original drafters. That makes sense for law enforcement officers, who should always try to figure out the lawmaker's intention, because under the separation of powers doctrine, the job of an enforcement officer is to carry out the legislative intent. However, interpreting the Constitution as originally intended enables regression because the Constitution was originally written by white Protestant men who deliberately left out everyone else.

To illustrate how the theory of originalism has been used as a means for taking us backward, I will offer the example of the Second Amendment and the rise of extremist modern militia movements.

The Second Amendment was drafted by enslavers who were afraid that a strong federal government would disarm or outlaw local militias. That was important to them because local militias were necessary to enforce the plantation system. The discussion about the need for the Second Amendment began in the Virginia State House when Virginian leaders were debating whether to ratify the Constitution.

George Mason, who was worried that the new Constitution gave the federal government control over armies and militias, said, "The militia may be here destroyed by that method which has been practiced in other parts of the world before; that is, by rendering them useless by disarming them." Without armed militias to control the enslaved population, these men knew just what would happen.

Patrick Henry noted that locally controlled militias were their "ultimate safety." He then reminded the group that slavery was "detested elsewhere" and suggested that the federal government's power to call up militias could be used to end slavery. He pointed out that the federal government could abolish slavery anytime by simply calling the states' Black men into military service and then setting them free. Others agreed.

The Second Amendment was drafted by James Madison, who attended that meeting in the Virginia State House. Here is the final form, as ratified:

> A well regulated Militia, being necessary to the security of a free State, the right of the people to keep and bear Arms, shall not be infringed.

For most of our history, the phrase "a well regulated Militia" was interpreted literally to mean that the states and local governments could organize militias.

The National Rifle Association (NRA) was founded in 1871 by Union Army General George Wingate and Colonel William C. Church, a journalist who volunteered to serve in the Union Army. They formed the NRA because they were appalled by the terrible marksmanship of Union soldiers. At the time, there was very little training for soldiers. They were expected to bring their own guns and come prepared to fight. Wingate and Church saw themselves as training and preparing future American soldiers. The NRA was thus founded as a gun safety and marksmanship training organization. For the first century of the NRA's existence, the organization was politically neutral, supporting both gun rights and certain gun safety regulations.

Then, in the 1970s, as the Civil Rights Movement gained momentum, the NRA underwent a significant ideological shift prompted by the changes. In 1977, a power struggle between the "old guard" and a more radical faction erupted in what has been called the 'Cincinnati Revolt.' The NRA leadership was taken over by a group that advocated for unrestricted access to firearms. They advanced the idea that the Second Amendment protected an individual's right to own guns, not just a collective right tied to militia service.

The modern militia movement was born in the early 1990s as a response to President Bill Clinton's gun control laws and the fatal shootouts at Ruby Ridge, Idaho, and Waco, Texas. The movement embraces what has been called the insurrection theory of the Second Amendment, which says that the Second Amendment protects the unconditional right to bear arms for self-defense—and that includes defense against a tyrannical government. According to this theory, when a government turns oppressive, private citizens have a duty to take up arms against the government. They point to the American Revolution to support the idea that citizens have the right to rebel against a tyrannical government. Thomas Jefferson, after all, once said that "a little rebellion now and then is a good thing."

Modern militias believe the federal government has become tyrannical. They look at the hundreds of alphabet-soup agencies generating volumes of rules and regulations limiting what they can do, and they look at the changing demographics, and conclude that the federal government no longer represents their interests. Instead, they believe the federal government is protecting outsiders or "others" at their expense.

White power militias put forward a theory called the "great replacement" or "white genocide theory," which holds that there is a deliberate plot to replace or diminish the power of white people in Western countries through non-white immigration. These militias are determined to fight against what they call white genocide.

In the words of Harvard political science professor Steven Levitsky:

Republican extremism is fueled by powerful pressure from below. The party's core constituents are white and Christian, and live in exurbs, small towns, and rural areas. Not only are white Christians in decline as a percentage of the electorate but growing diversity and progress toward racial equality have also undermined their relative social status.

According to a 2018 survey, nearly 60 percent of Republicans say they "feel like a stranger in their own country." Many Republican voters think the country of their childhood is being taken away from them.

Levitsky cited a 2021 survey sponsored by the American Enterprise Institute showing that an astonishing 56 percent of Republicans believe the "traditional American way of life is disappearing so fast that force may be necessary to save it."

That, too, is a response to the changes.

3
The Appeal
of Autocracy

Sociologist Max Weber in his classic essay "Politics as a Vocation" outlined three sources of authority that underlie governments. First is what he calls traditional authority, which underlies monarchies. Second is the rule of law, the authority underlying democracies. The third is what Weber calls a "charismatic leader." Today, we might say "strongman" or "demagogue." The strongman form of government draws its authority from the power and personality of the leader.

Thus, democracies draw their authority from laws that (in theory) bind all people equally. In a stable, rule-of-law democracy, change is slow. This is true given the very definition of *stable* which is "an object or structure not likely to give way or overturn." In addition, in a democracy based on rule of law, power is divided to prevent too much power from falling into the hands of a single person or small group of people. Dividing power leads to gridlock, and gridlock can be frustrating.

The difficulty of bringing about change in a stable democracy can lead people to seek more desperate means. Autocracy therefore holds appeal for those in a panic or who feel hopeless or helpless. The autocrat, who is unhampered by rules or gridlock, promises swift, dramatic action.

While the changes of the past seventy years were rapid in contrast to the previous 200 years, the changes occurred within the law and followed established procedures and what the Constitution allows. Moreover, the period of rapid changes was preceded by decades of grueling work on the parts of activists who laid the groundwork for civil rights. The work of activists and legal teams included reeducating judges and the population. By the time the changes came through the courts and legislation, a majority of Americans were ready to accept them. A poll in 1964, for example, found that 59 percent of Americans approved of the Civil Rights Act while 31 percent disapproved.

In contrast, the French Revolution of 1789 and the Russian Revolution of 1917 abruptly upended existing social and economic hierarchies. What we learn from these kinds of abrupt revolutions is that the outcome is unpredictable and not always what the revolutionaries wanted or intended.

The French revolutionaries not only toppled the monarchy and sought to eliminate the privileged class, but did so with swift and brutal violence. The goal of the French Revolution was to create a society based on reason and individual rights, with a government representing the will of the people. The utopian ideal included liberty, equality, and fraternity.

In what we may consider a historical irony, within fifteen years of the French Revolution, the French had a dictator. The reason is that upending the social and economic hierarchies created instability and factionalism. Napoleon came to power by essentially making two promises. He promised stability, and he promised to carry forward the ideals of the Revolution. He appealed to those who wanted order, and he appeased those who embraced the ideals of the Revolution, so he was able to pull together a large coalition. He did, in fact, take steps to equalize citizens. For example, it was Napoleon who decreed that Jewish citizens should have the full rights of citizenship. He also ruled as a dictator.

The Russian Revolution of 1917 was also carried out by radicals who sought to entirely upend the existing power and economic hierarchy. The goal of the Russian Revolution was to eliminate economic classes with a view to ending economic oppression. The revolutionaries envisioned a classless utopia.

It wasn't long before the Russian Revolution went completely off the rails. While the revolutionaries managed to get rid of the czar, they ended up with a totalitarian state. It was mostly Stalin's efforts to eliminate all opposition that led to a totalitarian state. The only way to eliminate all opposition is to exert complete control over the population, and because a great many people do not like to be controlled that way, it requires the use of force.

Stalin and his supporters justified his use of force and totalitarian methods as necessary to bring about the perfect utopian vision of a classless society. The inherent contradiction in using brutal violence against your own people to create a perfect society should have been obvious, but it wasn't.

Similarly, advocating rule-breaking in a rule-of-law society to save the rule of law is an inherent contradiction. Among other things, it undermines the authority that limits those in power.

Autocracy Promises Order

One appeal of autocracy is that it promises sameness. It reassures those who are afraid of differences.

People in an autocracy don't pull in different directions because it isn't permitted. Everyone knows their place. In an autocracy, you can feel reassured that others think as you do, and if they don't, they keep their views to themselves. For most people, life in an autocracy goes on. They get up in the morning, have their coffee, go to work, and take care of their families.

The differences are that, in an autocracy, you don't criticize the leader, you do what you are told to do, you believe (or pretend to believe) whatever you are told to believe, and you know that if you get into trouble, you cannot count on help from the government. People living in autocracies often avoid talking about politics altogether.

People imagine that autocracy will look like this:

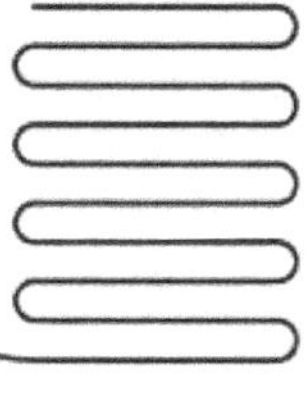

Here's the catch: Autocracies are not stable either. Eventually, autocracies topple. A personalist dictatorship has a particular vulnerability: uncertainty about the succession. In Russia, for example, nobody knows what will happen when Vladimir Putin dies. Personalist rulers often avoid designating a successor or creating a succession mechanism out of fear of losing control. They are afraid the successor will consolidate power while the personalist ruler is still alive. Not designating a successor keeps rivals uncertain and vying for the personalist ruler's favor.

Monarchies and family dynasties are more stable because the heir is the monarch's offspring, and the king can generally count on his own son or daughter not to bump him off to acquire power. Moreover, being the son or daughter of the king is lovely enough so that the heir is generally content to wait. Monarchy, however, has its own serious flaws. Suppose, for example, that the king's son is a nutcase.

A representative democracy, in theory, creates a meritocracy because the voters can—though often do not—vote for the most competent leaders.

Many of the Founders who called themselves anti-Federalists believed the lesson to be gleaned from the ancient democracies of Greece and Rome was that democracy thrives best when citizens share a common climate and culture. That is why many of them believed power should remain local.

Certainly, a small group of people who share a climate and culture will have less pushing and pulling than a large, sprawling, multicultural democracy. But, even with small groups, democracy is difficult. I was on a nonprofit board and there was much conflict. As the saying goes, if you put two people in a room, you will get three opinions.

There will always be a push and pull because people are different—with different desires and different fears. Even on a small, local scale, people push in different directions. If you don't believe me, run for local office and try to get something done. It took my community years to get a much-needed traffic light. Yes, many voters opposed the traffic light, even though they could see with their own eyes that people, including kids, waited for a break in the traffic and then darted across four lanes because they didn't want to walk a mile to the nearest light. (Can you guess which side of the traffic-light issue I was on?)

Whatever you suggest, no matter how sensible it seems to you, there will always be opposition. As Professor Andriy Chirovsky said, "Democracy is messy. Authoritarianism is neat." People who cannot tolerate the complexity, the messiness, and the give and take of democracy, long for order. They want all people to be the same.

That's why a large, complex, sprawling representative democracy like the United States, consisting of hundreds of separate jurisdictions and lots of bureaucracies to administer the regulations, looks like this:

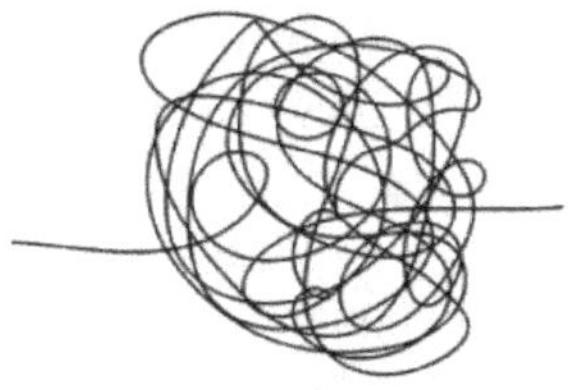

These are the same images I used earlier to illustrate "this is the world" and "this is the world with your brain on ideology," because autocracies and ideologies have much in common. For an autocracy to function, a controlling ideology is essential. Enough people must have an unshakable belief that the autocrat has special or perhaps divine powers to save the nation. Autocrats say things like "I, and I alone, can fix it."

The Appeal of Oligarchy

An oligarchy is a situation in which a small group of people have disproportionate power. Oligarchy is based on the idea that nature naturally forms a hierarchy. The strong and capable rise to the top.

Heather Cox Richardson, in her book, *How the South Won the Civil War,* points out that the United States has had two oligarchies, and we are currently slipping into a third.

The first oligarchy occurred during the plantation era, when one percent of the population—large plantation owners—controlled 90 percent of the nation's wealth and resources. The wealthy enslavers used their wealth and power to protect themselves. They believed that the hierarchy that put a few (white) men in charge was based on what they believed to be a fact of nature—superiority of the white race.

The Democratic Party, at that time, was the party of the Confederates and rural America. The Democrats wanted a limited federal government because they were afraid that the North, if given the chance, would end slavery. So they vetoed federal funds for infrastructure such as canals and highways because they understood that such infrastructure would strengthen the industrial North. Their argument was that the Constitution didn't give the federal government the power to do things like build highways across states.

The Constitution contains the Commerce Clause, which gives the federal government the power to regulate commerce among the states, but before the Civil War, the Commerce Clause mostly lay dormant. Those in power knew that invoking the Commerce Clause would alarm the South because if interpreted broadly it would give the federal government the authority to end slavery, which would lead to a Civil War.

In 1855 the Republican Party, called the Freedom Party, was born as an anti-slavery, pro-industry, pro-federal government party.

After the Civil War and the crushing defeat of the South, the Republicans had the power to pass pro-industry legislation. They built the kind of infrastructure—interstate highways and canals— that enabled industry to thrive. Republicans also gave us our first income tax.

As a result of the better infrastructure and pro-business legislation, we had an industrial revolution.

A few people who became known as business tycoons, or robber barons, grew wealthy. They often used ruthless business practices that were made possible because there were essentially no regulations.

They could fix prices, manipulate markets, and pay poverty wages. Because a few people had disproportionate wealth and power, the age of business tycoons was our second oligarchy.

The economic theory that allowed for this was called laissez-faire economics, or a free market economy. This theory holds that the economy works best when the government doesn't interfere. It's the idea that you just let it happen. What will be will be.

Free market proponents argued that personal liberty means that if a worker agrees to work ten hours for a few pennies, it's none of the government's business. They also argued that if employers offer bad working conditions, people will look for other jobs. Slavery, after all, was illegal, so the market would take care of the problem. In other words, they believed the government didn't have to, and shouldn't, do anything about unsafe or bad working conditions.

Free market proponents believe that taxing the wealthy to pay for welfare is simply stealing from the rich to give to the poor. They believe the wealthy should be *encouraged* to donate to charities—and many of the tycoons were also philanthropists—but free market proponents believe they should not be forced, or taxed.

This has been expressed as the makers and takers theory. The idea is that the makers are those who produce, and the takers are, to use author Ayn Rand's word, looters. Under this theory, welfare recipients are looters.

People on the lower end of the hierarchy often embrace this theory, which seems like a contradiction, but some people simply dislike regulations. They don't like being told what to do. Others hold to the theory that there is a natural hierarchy, therefore, attempts on the part of the government to create complete equality means going against nature. Perhaps some believe that they, or their children, will rise to the top.

The era from 1870 until the early 1900s has been called the Age of Business. Meanwhile, laborers worked long hours in dangerous jobs at poverty wages. There was no minimum wage, no forty-hour workweek, and no Social Security or worker protections, so while a few people became fabulously wealthy, most people labored in poverty.

At the beginning of the twentieth century, the Republican Party split into two factions: the pro-industry part and the pro-civil-rights portion that also became the pro-labor faction. By the 1920s, the pro-industry faction took control of the Republican Party. The Party dropped racial equality and labor issues from its platform and became the party of business.

The Democratic Party, at the time, consisted of former Confederates and agricultural America. Neither party during that period championed civil rights.

The Age of Business came tumbling down in 1929 when Wall Street crashed, followed by the Great Depression.

Enter, stage left, Franklin D. Roosevelt and his pro-labor New Deal. The New Deal offered worker protections, a minimum wage, and a forty-hour work week. That was when we got Social Security and worker protections. The G.I. Bill essentially educated a generation and moved a large number of people into the middle class.

As a result, the middle class strengthened. Income inequality came down, and we moved out of the second oligarchy.

Meanwhile, the parties continued shifting. Roosevelt drew many Black Americans into the Democratic coalition because they liked his pro-labor stance. Republicans, in contrast, pushed back against the pro-labor New Deal.

Beginning with President Truman, the Democratic Party began turning toward civil rights. As the Party embraced civil rights, many long-time Democrats, particularly those in the South, found themselves at odds with the Democratic Party. A group in the South called themselves Dixie Democrats, or Dixiecrats, who were opposed to things like integration.

At the same time, free-market proponents found that their economic policies were unpopular. People liked things such as social security and worker protections. To pull together a large coalition, Presidents Richard Nixon and Ronald Reagan invited the Dixiecrats into the Republican Party. The Party became the party of fiscal conservatives (people who were anti-regulation and against taxes) and social conservatives (people who didn't want to integrate, and blamed the women's movement for destroying what they called the traditional family).

What the two groups had in common was a dislike of the federal government and the new power that the federal government was taking on. Recall that the Civil Rights Movement largely happened through the United States Supreme Court and federal regulations.

By 1980, the Democratic Party had changed from the party of the Confederacy to the party of civil rights and urban America.

During the 1980 presidential election, which pitted Jimmy Carter against Ronald Reagan, I did some political polling. My job was to call the voters in a small town in Missouri, where I am originally from. I believe I called them all.

I had conversations like this:

> Me: What is your political affiliation?
>
> Town Resident: I'm a Democrat. My daddy was a Democrat, and my granddaddy was a Democrat.
>
> Me: Who will you be voting for, for president?
>
> Town Resident: Ronald Reagan.
>
> Me: But Reagan is a Republican and Carter is a Democrat.
>
> Town Resident: [laughs] I'm not voting for Carter.

In other words, I was watching the shift happen. At the local level, the more conservative candidates still called themselves Democrats. That, too, would soon change.

What has been called Reaganomics marked the beginning of a movement back toward deregulation. Reaganomics also meant tax cuts. Businesses benefited, but Reaganomics ushered in an era of increasing economic inequality. Today, income inequality is reaching levels like those in the 1920s, and we are edging toward our third oligarchy.

The election of Donald Trump in 2016 marked another shift of the Republican Party. Social conservatives who Presidents Ronald Reagan and Richard Nixon invited into the party, essentially took control. "Make America Great Again" is a reactionary call to arms.

Traditional fiscal conservatives who dislike Trump's demagoguery find themselves without a party. This suggests that another party realignment may be in our future.

There will always be a push and pull between those who view regulations as creating fairness and those who want to abolish regulations on the grounds that they interfere with personal liberty. For that matter, there will always be tension between one person's liberty to do as he or she pleases and another person's right not to be subjected to hurtful or damaging behavior. As the saying goes, your right to swing your fist stops where my nose begins. Drawing the line between regulations that create fairness and regulations that are burdensome and infringe on personal liberty with no tangible benefit is not easy.

Regulated Capitalism
Is the Best Economic System

I'll call this a theory, even though I think it's a fact: Regulated capitalism is the best economic system for today's world. Regulated capitalism offers the benefits of capitalism. Innovation is fostered, economic growth is promoted, and opportunities expand. Wider choices are available to consumers. Regulated capitalism generally brings a higher standard of living.

Regulating capitalism creates more fairness, which increases the benefits of capitalism by preventing things such as market manipulation, insider trading, false advertising, and worker exploitation. If cheating isn't allowed, genuine innovation is encouraged. The prize then goes to true innovators instead of those who figure out how to manipulate and cheat others. Regulation allows more freedom and opportunity because more people can participate.

However, as you would expect, some capitalists don't want to be regulated. Companies will frequently come out on the side of profits over the public good. "We will make less profit, but the general population will benefit," I assume, is rarely the consensus of a corporate board of directors.

So there is a constant push and pull between those who want industry to be regulated and those who think the economy works best when it is unregulated. That adds another element to the constant flux and vulnerability of democratic forms of government.

Democracy Requires Compromise

Recall the Pinochet story and what Harvard Professors Steven Levitsky and Daniel Ziblatt said about mutual tolerance. When the opposing parties in a democracy refuse to compromise and prioritize winning at all costs, democracy is in danger of breaking down. This is particularly true when one side resorts to illegal means.

Some people don't want to compromise. They want things their way. Those people will never feel comfortable in a democratic government based on the rule of law. They will insist on their way, they will refuse to compromise, and they will advocate rule-breaking to save the system. Such people, if they accumulate too much power, will derail a democratic form of government.

A Large, Sprawling, Diverse, Multicultural Democracy Is Always in Danger

What we might call the existence pain of democracies is that they are always difficult. James Madison wrote, "If men were angels, no government would be necessary." If we were angels, democracy would also work perfectly—but then, we wouldn't need a government in the first place.

The existence pain of democracy includes knowing that our world is messy, imperfect, and in constant flux. It means knowing and accepting that democracy is never easy. People are imperfect, and democracy means "rule by the people," so democracy can never work perfectly. Those who want perfection and cannot tolerate the constant flux will reject democracy.

Recall Karen Stenner's theory that the worldwide rise of authoritarian movements has happened because liberal democracy has exceeded many people's capacity to tolerate it.

Until recently in our evolutionary history, humans were concerned only with their immediate surroundings. The world was a simpler place. Humans knew that large predatory cats were dangerous, they knew that the neighboring group might make war on them, and they knew which berries were good to eat. Today, our lives are interconnected with people who live on the other side of the planet.

Evolutionary biologists and neuroscientists tell us that our brains are poorly equipped to cope with globalization. Put another way, our technology is in danger of outpacing our wisdom to manage it.

If life or democracy is hard, a person may look for someone to blame. Such people are vulnerable to the siren call of a demagogue. A person who can't hold a job as a casual laborer may be taught to blame immigrants for taking his job. A man continually rejected by women can be taught to blame the changes that have made women independent.

Liberals and progressives are always introducing new ideas or trying to improve what is there, while conservatives resist change. Regressives feel that something is being lost and try to undo the changes. Even people who are mostly liberal can start feeling like "Okay, now things have gone too far." There may be more people like that than we realize because they may be afraid to say how they feel.

Consider these messages:

- People are coming to take our jobs.

- People less qualified than us are taking our jobs, and it

isn't fair.

- What is essentially American is being lost.

- The cities are teeming with crime, immorality, and vice.

- We are being invaded by foreigners who want to change America into something else.

These messages in the hands of a skillful demagogue can ignite a reactionary movement.

Some people who respond to the above messages may have a vague feeling of unease, discomfort, or fear without understanding the source of those fears and anxieties. Things may have moved too quickly, so they may be uncomfortable. They are uneasy with all this stuff about gender and pronouns.

These kinds of messages, which play on fears that come from rapid changes, can send a person into an ideological spiral.

You've Got to Be
Carefully Taught

We turn back now to the artists because artists can impart wisdom in a way that resonates deeply. That is partly because artists express their messages through symbols, metaphors, or stories. Art, after all, is condensed life.

The musical *South Pacific* tackled the issue of racism in 1949. When the play was first performed on Broadway, racial segregation was legal. The modern Civil Rights Movement was in the future.

The story is about how people often initially resist what is new and different. One of the main characters, Nellie, overcomes her prejudice after she spends time with people who are different, and becomes comfortable with them.

There was pressure on Rodgers and Hammerstein to remove the song, "You've Got to Be Carefully Taught," because it was considered too controversial. James Michener, the author of the book on which the play was based, later recalled that Rodgers and Hammerstein "replied stubbornly that the number represented why they wanted to do the play, and that even if it meant failure of the production, it was going to stay in."

The song so offended some lawmakers that they introduced a bill to outlaw entertainment having "an underlying philosophy inspired by Moscow." By that, they meant communism. And by that, they meant going against what they believed was essentially American.

The character says, "It is not born in you! It happens after you are born!" The song he then sings includes these lyrics:

> You've got to be taught to hate and fear.
> You've got to be taught from year to year . . .
> To hate all the people your relatives hate,
> You've got to be carefully taught.

You can find the original performance from the movie version by searching on YouTube for "You've Got to Be Carefully Taught."

You've got to be carefully taught is exactly what the neuroscientists also tell us. For an ideology to take root, it must be continually reinforced.

However, as people become accustomed to changes, what was once new and scary becomes familiar and comfortable. People who embrace change and are comfortable with the new and different perhaps need to show patience to those who need time to adjust.

Psychiatrist M. Scott Peck, on the first page of his book, *The Road Less Traveled*, said this:

> Life is difficult. This is a great truth, one of the greatest truths. It is a great truth because once we truly see this truth, we transcend it. Once we truly know that life is difficult—once we truly understand and accept it—then life is no longer difficult. Because once it is accepted, the fact that life is difficult no longer matters.

His idea is that once we understand that life is difficult, we stop moaning about it and get to work solving problems as they arise.

The same can be said about democracy. Democracy is always difficult. Once we understand this, we stop being shocked each time there is a setback and set to work looking for solutions.

4
Rage
Merchants

Political extremists and would-be autocrats are not the only people who benefit from inciting panic and fear. There is big money to be made in peddling powerful emotions. *The Music Man's* Harold Hill, after all, wasn't interested in power. He wanted to earn a quick buck. In the world of the Internet and social media, skillfully inciting or inflaming panic and outrage can bring an ordinary person wealth and fame.

And you are the target. Some people take the bait. Others tune out the noise and disengage from politics entirely, which creates a new problem: widespread apathy. The ideal response is to filter out the noise and engage with politics in a more productive way. But that's not easy, particularly when the demagogues are deliberately trying to trigger panic.

Panic is a sudden, intense reaction to a threat in the environment. It is a basic, primal emotion rooted in the evolutionary older parts of the brain and linked to survival and self-preservation. Panic triggers a fight-or-flight response. For most of our evolutionary history, we lived in proximity to predators. If a cave dweller was out gathering nuts and berries and heard a threatening noise, panic would get the cave dweller to safety. Panic can therefore serve a useful purpose.

One evening, a raccoon came over the fence and got into a fight with our 12-pound terrier. I had about one second to respond. I dashed outside and shouted to startle the animals, which gave them a moment to separate. I then did something I would have never thought I could do. I picked up a large, plastic Adirondack chair, lifted it over my head, and hurled it at the raccoon. I don't know whether the chair hit him or just scared him, but while the chair was still bouncing on the patio, the raccoon scrambled over the fence and ran away.

The dog required a visit to the vet for stitches and shots. Years later, I still tell the story in disbelief. "I threw a chair at a raccoon!" I am a very small human being. I was able to hurl that chair and aim accurately because I was in a panic and focused on the emergency, which meant I didn't have time to think about what I was doing. Panic and adrenaline saved my dog, who should have selected flight over fight, but try explaining that to a terrier who probably thought *he* saved the day.

Panic is useful in the face of immediate danger. There is no time to think, and overthinking an emergency can lead to paralysis. That's why demagogues try to send people into a panic. A person in a panic does not reason well because rational thought is impaired. If you told me, "Throw this chair at that raccoon" and there was no immediate danger, I'd refuse.

On the other hand, when confronted with a fight between a raccoon and the family dog, this would not be the appropriate response:

When it comes to political matters, we're usually dealing with events beyond our direct experience. Effective responses rely on the rational and deliberate parts of the brain. Civilians of an occupied country cannot mount an effective resistance while in the throes of panic. An effective resistance requires a cool head and strategic planning. The leaders who have done the most to improve our world thought strategically, a feat impossible when panic takes over.

Anger, like panic, is a primal emotion rooted in survival instincts. While panic triggers a fight-or-flight response, anger readies a person to confront danger head on.

Outrage is different. Outrage engages more evolved parts of the brain associated with social interactions, moral reasoning, and concepts of justice. Outrage brings in a sense of fairness and moral judgment. Outrage is more contagious and prolonged than anger. It has a group-oriented, public-facing nature, often aligning with collective calls for justice.

Wait, you may be thinking. *Aren't calls for justice good for democracy?*

Calls for justice can be good for democracy, and outrage can lead to positive social reform. Outrage can also lead someone to justify rule-breaking. It can lead people to justify cruelty. It can lead to revolution, violence, and unpredictable outcomes. Unless the goal is to destroy an existing power structure or start an actual war, prolonged collective outrage is risky.

Moreover, people who experience extended fear and outrage are at risk of going into ideological spirals. Continual outrage, particularly when coming from multiple sources, can turn people against each other and set up the kind of chaos that demagogues and would-be dictators can use for their benefit.

Information Revolutions
Enable Rage Merchanting

The first information revolution in modern history was the invention of the printing press. The second was the Internet. Both revolutions allowed misinformation, disinformation, and destructive rage to spread at dangerous levels.

In 1455, after Gutenberg invented the printing press and printed his first book, a Latin-language Bible, he reportedly said, "God's word shall be carried far and wide."

God's word was not the only thing carried far and wide.

Before the invention of the printing press, people got their news from town criers, who were appointed by local authorities. Their job was to announce new decrees, laws, and important events. Written letters were another source of news, but they were almost exclusively exchanged between scholars and members of the upper classes who had the leisure to write letters. Book ownership was limited to those with wealth. Written material disseminated to the public had to be painstakingly copied by hand. The average person was not confronted with written material on a large scale until the invention of the printing press.

Broadsides, which became common after the invention of the printing press, were papers printed on one side and distributed widely. They often contained important news and information, but just as often, they spread destructive lies and malicious gossip to a population untrained in evaluating the reliability of sources. When broadsides were first distributed, unsubstantiated rumors flew. Political unrest was fomented.

While the printing press didn't cause the Protestant Reformation, it was the most important driver of it because it allowed the reformist ideas to be disseminated at an unprecedented speed and scale. People swept up in the moment took to the streets in anger. The church also tended to respond too quickly and in too heavy-handed a manner. All this ignited violence and religious wars that fractured Europe for centuries.

Similarly, the invention of the printing press was a pivotal factor in allowing the conspiracy theory of blood libel to spread widely across Europe. This was the conspiracy theory that Jewish people murdered Christian children to use their blood in making Passover matzos.

Eventually, people learned to evaluate written sources. Once books and reputable publications became widely available, consumers of news came to understand that a broadside nailed to a tree very likely had less credibility than a book or publication by a respected scholar and publisher.

Yellow Journalism

Newspaper reading became widespread between the seventeenth and nineteenth centuries as literacy rates rose.

By the late nineteenth century, news outlets were competing for readers. Publishers in need of readers discovered that sensational and rage-inducing material sold more newspapers and magazines, which gave rise to a style of news coverage known as yellow journalism. This new form of journalism emphasized sensationalism, bold headlines, and creative presentation over facts.

Yellow journalism reached its peak in 1898 after the United States deployed the USS *Maine* to Havana in a show of U.S. military power. On February 15, 1898, an explosion sank the ship. The initial report from the Cuban colonial government, confirmed by witnesses, was that the explosion occurred onboard. Both William Randolph Hearst and his rival Joseph Pulitzer had been fueling anti-Spanish sentiment to sell newspapers. Following the sinking of the *Maine*, both Hearst and Pulitzer published inflammatory rumors, stirring public outrage with accusations of a Spanish plot to destroy the ship.

Eventually, there was a public reaction against yellow journalism. This prompted the rise of a new kind of reporting that was serious and fact-based. Tabloids continued, but eventually they were relegated to racks at the supermarket and were widely known to be mostly—if not entirely—fiction.

From the 1940s until the 1980s, there was only a handful of mass-market media outlets. As a result, media producers sought to appeal to as wide a swath of the American public as possible typically by offering viewers what NBC vice president Paul Klein called "the least objectionable programming." Programming was neutral, calm, and factual. Broadcasts and major publications reached a large enough audience so no attempt was made to sensationalize the news. Sets were boring. Anchors like Walter Cronkite recited facts.

The three major broadcast networks—ABC, CBS, and NBC— were subsidized from commercial advertisements and the profits from highly rated prime-time dramas. The evening news was thus available to anyone with a television set. People in that era typically received their news once or twice a day, either through a morning or evening newspaper or via the evening broadcast. At the same time, large circulations and revenue from advertisers kept the price of newspapers low. Consumers absorbed the day's news and then went about their business.

Media reporting from the 1940s through the 1960s fueled some of the rapid changes I've talked about in the era beginning in the 1950s. Iconic images disseminated widely in the media included the body of Emmett Till, a fourteen-year-old boy lynched in Mississippi. Another photograph captured Elizabeth Eckford, a fifteen-year-old girl taunted by an angry white mob as she attempted to attend Central High School after the school was ordered to integrate following the Supreme Court's 1954 decision in *Brown v. Board of Education.*

These images were seen by a great many people who had never fully considered civil rights issues. Suddenly, their sympathy—and yes, their outrage—was aroused. Because those images shocked the conscience of a significant portion of the population, the media coverage helped galvanize nationwide support for civil rights.

Although the goal was neutral reporting, social conservatives complained that their views were not being represented in the mainstream media. Given this, it may seem surprising that conservatives were responsible for abolishing the Fairness Doctrine, which required, among other things, that broadcast networks devote time to contrasting views on issues of public importance. However, some fiscal conservatives believed that producers should be allowed to include whatever they wanted and should not be compelled to go against their judgment by federal regulations. In 1985, FCC chairman Mark S. Fowler, a lawyer who had served on President Reagan's campaign staff, released a report stating that the doctrine hurt the public interest and violated the free speech rights guaranteed by the First Amendment. The idea was that broadcasters should be allowed to do what they please.

We know from the *Zenger* trial in 1735 that freedom of the press was one of the founding conditions. It is therefore not surprising that conservatives would jealously guard that particular freedom.

The FCC's report that the Fairness Doctrine violated the First Amendment was controversial, including among some conservatives, who argued that the Fairness Doctrine was the only thing that kept networks from lambasting Reagan's economic policies. But the FCC panel voted to repeal the Fairness Doctrine. Congress, which was in the hands of Democrats, passed a bill to prevent this, but Reagan vetoed the bill. Reagan, like Fowler, believed that the Fairness Doctrine represented a form of control and censorship over what media outlets could do.

The Return of
Yellow Journalism

Less than one year after the Fairness Doctrine was repealed, Rush Limbaugh launched his radio show. He presented himself as a conservative alternative to mainstream media. He was also an entertainer. In his words, "I happen to have great entertainment skills." He was intentionally incendiary, making comments like these: "Feminism was established so as to allow unattractive women access to the mainstream of society," and "Have you ever noticed how all composite pictures of wanted criminals resemble Jesse Jackson?"

He soon amassed a large audience and earned tens of millions of dollars annually. At the peak of his career in the 1990s, he had an estimated 20 million listeners. In 2018, *Forbes* listed his income as $84.5 million.

Much of Limbaugh's audience used his show as their primary source for news, marking the start of media fragmentation. The fracturing of the media market accelerated in the late 1990s with the introduction of cable news networks: CNN, Fox News, and MSNBC. Keeping in mind the limitations of political spectrums, I will refer to Fox News as targeting right-wing audiences and MSNBC as targeting left-wing audiences. They are known as partisan news shows. If we understand "news" to mean "factual"—or as close to factual as possible given that biases necessarily creep in—the label "partisan news" is a contradiction in terms.

Something like this happened before. During the Partisan Press Era (1790s to 1820s), the idea of journalistic objectivity did not exist. The Federalist Party, one of the two major political parties at the time, controlled its own newspaper. Meanwhile, the Democratic-Republicans, the other major party, controlled a different newspaper. To stay informed, people read both newspapers, contrasted the views, and decided where they stood.

The rise of cable news programs created a twenty-four-hour news cycle, which meant lots of time to fill. Meanwhile, news itself had to be made profitable because cable news shows didn't have revenue from successful sitcoms to subsidize news reporting. To generate revenue, cable news shows had to find a way to keep viewers glued to the screen. Sets became glitzy. Hosts became performers. To hold the attention of audiences, cable news introduced what Dannagal Goldthwaite Young, in her book *Wrong! How Media, Politics and Identity Drive Our Appetite for Misinformation*, calls the partisan pundit. She says this:

> The phenomenon of the "partisan pundit" is a useful television (especially cable) news routine that embraces the conflict frame while offering emotionally evocative performances of partisan identity. Pundits are talking heads who appear on the news not to "report" news but to talk about the news.

> Cable news programs frequently assemble panels of pundits (for example, journalists, experts, and partisan commentators) who argue about the topic, tie that topic to broad themes in the culture war, and typically do so with the "in your face" interpersonal conflict style that increases viewer engagement while also increasing viewers' hostility toward the other side.

Young describes the characteristics of TV pundits like this:

> Pundit panels are characterized by performances of intellectual arrogance or "I am not listening because I just want to show I'm right." Intellectual arrogance plays well on television, whereas intellectual humility does not. In fact, we rarely see intellectual humility modeled in our mediated political world. When we do, it's from the occasional appearance of scientists—people trained to never prove things or remove themselves from doubt. They don't speak in absolutes or forevers. They speak with caveats and conditions and often answer with "Time will tell" and "for now this seems to be the case."

Intellectual arrogance is one of the markers that distinguishes ideological thinkers from those with more flexible thinking. Those with intellectual humility are more flexible thinkers. The problem is that intellectual humility isn't entertaining. "Give me a minute to think about that" followed by a deep contemplative silence is boring. On the other hand, watching people argue and pound tables with their fists can be riveting.

Not all commentators who appear on cable news deliver bias-confirming, emotionally evocative performances. That would be predictable and boring. There are balanced and thoughtful commentaries. Scholars are often invited on the shows. Some regular commentators are thoughtful and measured, but it's the emotionally laden performances that are most memorable. Neuroscience explains why. The amygdala, the emotion processor in the brain, becomes highly active during a rage-filled performance. That releases stress hormones such as noradrenaline and glucocorticoids that "tag" the experience as important for long-term storage. Calm, nuanced performances, on the other hand, fade because the brain treats them as less significant.

Partisan pundits now include a new category of show people: TV lawyers. Peter Arenella, a UCLA law professor emeritus and one of the first TV legal pundits for ABC news, wrote a piece that appeared in the *University of Chicago Legal Forum* in 1998 called "The Perils of TV Legal Punditry." In it, he delivered a scathing account of how TV lawyers are entertainers who must "evoke strong emotions in the audience." Arenella saw that outlets needed viewers, so they needed to provide content that would sustain readership and viewership. They therefore needed pundits who were willing to speculate and put forward gripping theories. Arenella later offered this mea culpa (which I am quoting with his permission):

I worked for a major network in the 1990s. I started by commenting on high-profile Los Angeles criminal cases —Rodney King, McMartin, Menendez brothers, and OJ's criminal/civil trials. I either attended these trials, or I closely observed them. The network wanted to expand my role by using me to comment on national high-profile criminal cases that I had not watched. These were cases where I could only rely on media accounts by lay journalists who did not understand the legal complexities involved. I took the work.

My reckoning came when impeachment charges were filed against President Clinton for lying about a sexual affair with one of his staff. A producer wanted me to debate Alan Dershowitz, my former teacher at Harvard Law School. Initially, I refused. I pointed out that, as a professor of criminal law, my expertise was not in our impeachment history, which meant I would be commenting as a private citizen. My producer replied, "Peter, our demographics show that our viewers see you as a more objective academic with no particular political interest in the outcome of this process."

To my regret, I did that interview. That was when I realized I had fallen prey to the seductive power of being anointed a "national expert" on all legal issues. Embarrassed by my decision to do that interview, I quit my ABC consulting position and returned to my real passion: teaching and writing about important and troubling criminal law issues.

When I started working for ABC News, I naively believed that I could educate the viewing audience about complex criminal law issues. What I learned is that TV legal commentary usually legitimates whatever TV producers view as the current audience consensus about some high-profile case. Instead of educating the public, far too much televised legal commentary simply serves as a mirror that reflects back to its particular audience what it already believes.

What Arenella describes is programming that confirms the viewers' pre-existing biases, which neuroscientists tell us is both pleasurable and addictive. Cognitive bias is the term for the tendency to seek out and favor information that confirms a person's existing beliefs. Information that confirms our beliefs can trigger the release of dopamine, the "feel-good" neurotransmitter. Having our biases confirmed feels good, so we want more.

Tufts University professors Jeffrey Berry and Sarah Sobieraj, authors of *The Outrage Industry: Political Opinion Media and the New Incivility,* explain that what they call the outrage industry—which includes cable news programs, political blogs, and talk radio—encourages "agent provocateurs," a phenomenon that was a nearly unthinkable risk in the era of the least objectionable programming. Rush Limbaugh, an agent provocateur, was obviously not interested in attracting a wide audience. He was interested in captivating and keeping his niche audience, which was large enough to allow him to charge high rates to advertisers.

Dannagal Goldthwaite Young cites a *New York Times* piece about Fox News' internal "minute-by-minute rating data." The data, which record real-time audience ebb and flow, allowed Tucker Carlson, who hosted a nightly political talk show from 2016 to 2023, to adjust his script as the show was in progress to get the most reaction from his audience. His goal was to trigger strong emotional responses.

A 2013 Pew Research Center study found that 85 percent of MSNBC's programming was commentary or opinion. Fox News did better with 55 percent commentary or opinion and 45 percent factual reporting. CNN was more balanced, with 46 percent commentary and 54 percent factual reporting.

The problem, of course, as confirmed in a 2024 study by Jeffrey J. Mondak, a professor of political science, is that many Americans have a difficult time distinguishing fact from opinion. That means a great many Americans are getting opinions about the news but think they are getting facts. What they are getting are bias-confirming and rage-inducing performances.

This study also found that political leanings influenced what people believe to be facts as opposed to opinion. In the words of Professor Mondak, "As partisan political views grow more polarized, Democrats and Republicans both tend to construct an alternate reality in which they report that their side has marshaled the facts and the other side merely has opinions." In other words, what psychologists call confirmation bias is at work.

Popular cable news hosts achieve star status. In the words of Berry and Sobieraj, "Unlike a conventional news program, in which the news itself is central, and anchors are often replaced, there would be no *Rachel Maddow Show* without Rachel Maddow."

These hosts are not reporters. They do not break news. "Instead, they reinterpret, reframe, and unpack news from the headlines, political speeches, or claims made by other outrage hosts." News reporters earn about $60,000 per year. After taking a pay cut in 2024, Rachel Maddow earned $25 million annually.

MSNBC hosts sometimes repeat for their audiences what someone over there at Fox said. The Fox quotations generally come from Fox agent provocateurs and are selected for the MSNBC audience for outrage purpose. In other words, the most outrageous claims will be selected.

Right-wing media will do the same thing. A right-wing host will select something said by a left-wing agent provocateur, which leads right-wing viewers to believe that everyone on the left is completely unhinged.

That not only outrages the target audience, but also leads the audience to believe that all people on the other side hold the same outrageous view. Keep in mind that the sizes of these cable news audiences are relatively small. At its height, MSNBC had about three million viewers. Fox has drawn audiences as large as seven million. That's a lot of people, but not relative to the 174 million people who voted in the 2024 election. In addition, these audiences are mostly people of retirement age. The median age of the CNN, Fox, and MSNBC audiences is, respectively, 67, 68, and 71. Thus, portraying all voters as holding the most outrageous views presented on Fox or MSNBC is misleading.

Conspiracy Theories

Dannagal Goldthwaite Young explains how the current media environment is driving an appetite for conspiracy theories. She offers this definition of a conspiracy theory:

> Conspiracy theories are allegations that remain unsubstantiated. They attempt to explain the ultimate causes of significant social and political events and circumstances with claims of secret plots by two or more powerful actors. They also assume that powerful people operating in the shadows are bad actors deliberately keeping the public in the dark.

Young describes how conspiracy theories evolve:

- People face a situation that is confusing or seems incomprehensible.

- They look for a way to assign blame.

- They grasp onto an easy-to-understand theory that assigns blame.

- The theory will be reinforced if people in their community and people they identify with (or look to as an authority) also hold the theory.

- Holding a conspiracy theory gives them a renewed sense of energy. Instead of feeling out of control, they have an explanation.

- Fueled by anger, they become defiant—but they have a direction. They feel they have agency. They can get behind a banner. They feel back in control.

Notice that a conspiracy theory doesn't have to be unhinged. It doesn't have to be about faked moon landings or implanting microchips in vaccines. It simply needs to assign blame for a confusing situation. Also, notice that conspiracy theories arise when people face a situation that is confusing or seems incomprehensible. The modern world of globalism is confusing to a lot of people. Our legal system has grown so complex that most people do not understand it. The complexity of the modern world, therefore, gives rise to conspiracy theories.

Young makes clear that conspiracy theories arise in both left-leaning and right-leaning media ecosystems. Berry and Sobieraj agree that outlets that target left-wing audiences and outlets that target right-wing audiences use the same tactics, but Berry and Sobieraj say this:

> Our data indicate that the right uses decidedly more outrage speech than the left. Taken as a whole, liberal content is quite nasty in character, following the outrage model with accusations, conspiracy theories, and ridicule. Conservatives, however, are even nastier.

Right-wing media is better at all things outrage, including making money. Back when Rush Limbaugh was earning $59 million annually, liberal outrage manufacturers were only in the single-digit millions.

Enter Stage Right, the Performance Master of Outrage,
Donald Trump

Into this environment came Donald Trump, a product of the current media environment. Before running for President, he was a reality TV show host. He therefore understands how this all works. Among the things he understands is that the way to get more media coverage is to be as outrageous as possible. Remember that Trump is not conservative. He doesn't want to conserve anything. He wants change, and he wants it fast. He therefore benefits from continually stoking outrage. He pulls people into an outrage cycle that looks like this:

- He does something outrageous that shocks or enrages his critics.

- The same act thrills his supporters because it carries symbolic significance. The act, in some form, lands a blow on the liberal establishment.

- When his critics exhibit a strong reaction, his supporters feel an even greater thrill because he is proving he can take on the enemy. "Trump is a radical," they say approvingly. "He is upsetting the applecart. He is fighting for us."

- Meanwhile, Trump keeps himself center stage and controls the conversation.

Trump enlarged the public appetite for news. People before Trump who had never followed the ups and downs of politics tuned in and remained glued to their screens to see what outrageous thing he would do next.

In 2015, MSNBC had 132,000 prime-time viewers. Then Trump happened, and MSNBC experienced a bonanza. By 2020, MSNBC had a whopping 2.2 million viewers. Overnight, MSNBC cable news hosts became left-wing heroes. Their social media followings skyrocketed. Social media influencers who nobody had ever heard of before were born, spreading outrage over Trump's latest antics and quickly amassing large followings. This has been called the Trump Bump. Former CBS executive Les Moonves said this about Trump's impact on ratings during the early stages of the 2016 election cycle: "It may not be good for America, but it's damn good for CBS."

New online media outlets were created to feed the sudden appetite for news. These new outlets didn't break news; they aggregated news that someone else broke. Some news outlets and accounts did nothing but offer minute-by-minute reporting of each outrageous thing Trump did or said.

Notice what is happening: Media markets are fragmenting into smaller and smaller units. As media markets fragment, outlets compete for viewers, and we have the rise of a new and improved form of yellow journalism.

It was common in left-leaning circles to mock Trump's word salads and indecorous behavior. He wrote in all caps on social media. He talked in circles. How, his critics wondered, did such a figure of absurdity become President?

In *Demagogue for President: The Rhetorical Genius of Donald Trump*, Texas A&M University professor Jennifer Mercieca stood against the crowd of Trump-mockers and argued that Trump's gaffes are not gaffes. She pointed out, for example, that he effectively uses a device known as ad populum ("appeal to the crowd") by deliberately positioning his lack of political correctness as genuineness. He positions speaking in a manner acceptable to the mainstream as being "scripted," which he then equates with going along with corruption. The result is that the more outrageous his comments, the more "truthful" he appears to his supporters and the more they admire him.

A Trump supporter told me once, in an approving tone, that Trump "tells it like it is." I asked, "He tells *what* like it is?" She turned away. She didn't have to say it aloud because Trump was saying it for her.

Maybe, just maybe, Trump is fooling his critics who think he's a fool.

5
Social Media
Makes It Worse

The Internet, the second major information revolution after the printing press, did more than simply facilitate the spread of misinformation and disinformation. It transformed how people communicate. It also revolutionized how news is transmitted.

Because the cost of producing and distributing information is falling close to zero, people are deluged with choices of what to pay attention to. A person with a Substack account that costs $5 per month per subscription can earn $10,000 per month with only 2,000 subscribers. The only requirement is to write content that appeals to—and hooks—a few thousand people. Where once CBS, NBC, ABC, and major newspapers aimed for neutrality to reach as large an audience as possible, audiences are now broken down into numbers as small as a few thousand. These smaller outlets, therefore, have an incentive to affirm the biases of their audiences.

According to the Pew Research Center, in 2024, nearly a third of all consumers of news got their news "often" from social media. An additional 24 percent get their news "sometimes" from social media. That encourages tailoring news and commentary to fit narrow tastes and specific demands.

Social media as a source of news has created a phenomenon known as ideological filter bubbles built through algorithms. An Internet algorithm draws on vast amounts of user data to predict and deliver the content each person is most likely to find engaging. The term "filter bubble" was first coined by Eli Pariser in his 2011 book, *The Filter Bubble: What the Internet Is Hiding from You*. He showed that when a person searches for information online, algorithms show users personalized content based on their online behavior, such as search history, location, and past clicks. That means users are shown information that aligns with their existing beliefs and interests, thereby reinforcing those views. This is getting worse as artificial intelligence gets better at telling people what they want to hear and confirming their biases.

The Pew Research Center has found that nearly all the content people see on social media is chosen, not by human editors, but rather by algorithms. On a social media platform, the algorithm will suggest other people to follow based on who the user already follows and the kind of content the user engages with. That is how people end up in ideological filter bubbles, which are highly efficient conspiracy-theory, rage-generating machines. They work like this:

- Person A sees a misleading headline or a headline stating an opinion as if it is a fact.

- Person A clicks on it, skims the article without reading closely, thereby missing the subtlety. The person clicks "like."

- The algorithm shows Person A lots of like-minded partisans talking about the opinion in the article as if it is a fact.

- The algorithm then shows the person a "legal expert" commenting approvingly on the misleading headline. The algorithm is smart enough to show a "legal expert" who shares Person A's political views. (I have learned that every lawyer becomes a legal expert on social media. In real life, there are good lawyers, mediocre lawyers, and bad lawyers. On social media and cable news, all are legal experts.)

- Over the coming days, weeks, months, or even longer, members of Person A's community continually reinforce her beliefs.

Person A is simply a misinformed person. Multiply Person A by hundreds of thousands or even millions of people in an ideological filter bubble, and you have a situation.

In a *60 Minutes* interview, Facebook whistleblower Frances Haugen explained that "angry content" on Facebook is more likely to receive engagement. She said that content producers and political parties are aware of this. In her testimony before Congress, she said that Facebook algorithms deliberately incentivize angry, polarizing content. Social media users who want to amass a large following in political filter bubbles learn quickly that content that either confirms the biases of their audiences or generates anger will bring them more engagement.

Social media algorithms create conflict by elevating material that promotes division and creates rage. Platformer learned that X (formerly Twitter) under Musk's leadership, maintained a list of around thirty-five VIP users whose accounts it monitors and offers increased visibility. The list includes the following:

- *Daily Wire* founder and conservative commentator Ben Shapiro

- Pseudonymous conservative commentator @catturd2

- Rep. Alexandria Ocasio-Cortez (D-NY)

As observers have noted, figures like Ben Shapiro and @Catturd2 enrage the left. Alexandria Ocasio-Cortez enrages the right. Elevating these users stimulates engagement by riling people. Getting people fighting is profitable for X's revenue stream.

There is a thing on X called dunking. The dunkee says something outrageous or painfully stupid. The dunker reposts the statement and dunks on it by adding a clever or snarky statement intended to highlight the outrageousness or stupidity of the statement. This works best if the dunkee is a public figure.

Both sides think they win a dunking contest. The dunker shows how clever he or she is, and the dunkee gets to be the star of a show entitled *Watch Me Trigger the Enemy.* The dunking game drives up partisanship and increases engagement.

The left-wing media ecosystem and the right-wing ecosystem have been erroneously called echo chambers. An echo chamber implies that people in each ecosystem are only exposed to views from their own side. In fact, audiences in each ecosystem are continually shown the views of the other side. After all, that's what dunking is all about.

Leor Zmigrod compares online political communities to life in a "tightly controlled propagandist state." She says this:

> Take a vulnerable mind—sensitive to negative information and threats, cognitively rigid, impulsive— and place this mind in an environment that selectively preys on these biases, and it becomes possible to understand why these spaces, though toxic for everyone, are especially toxic for people who are at baseline already psychologically vulnerable. The more technology obfuscates the source, truth, and reliability of images, texts, videos, and reports, the more likely it is that digital environments will be radicalizing spaces.

The current incendiary media environment, which activates the authoritarian instincts of people while vilifying people on the other "side," does something more sinister than simply exacerbate the polarization. Recall the words of Judge Learned Hand:

> The spirit of liberty is the spirit which is not too sure that it is right; the spirit of liberty is the spirit which seeks to understand the minds of other men and women.

People whose fears and rage are continually activated in this manner become less free and less humane. They are being carefully taught to hate and fear.

The Other Divide

In *The Other Divide: Polarization and Disengagement in American Politics* (2022), authors Yanna Krupnikov, professor of political science and communication, and John Barry Ryan, political scientist, argue that the main division in US politics isn't between the left and the right. It's between a relatively small group of vocal hyper-partisans and the larger group who have elected to tune out the noise.

Krupnikov and Ryan divide Americans into three groups. The first group is uninvolved in politics. They pay no attention, and they generally don't vote. The second group focuses on politics when something is important to them, and they vote. The third group—the vocal hyper-partisans—dominate the landscape. They also genuinely dislike rank-and-file members of the opposing party. Some members of the third group even wish ill on out-partisans. In contrast, people in the first and second groups may dislike the policies of some opposing party leaders, but they bear no ill will against people who vote for the opposing party.

Because these vocal, deeply involved hyper-partisans attract disproportionate attention, this group wields an outsized influence on how Americans perceive politics.

Krupnikov and Ryan dispel the popular notion that the outrage industry is a result of polarization. They argue instead that the outrage industry arose because it was profitable, but it has exacerbated the problem of polarization.

All of this is damaging what sociologists call the public sphere, a place where citizens come together to exchange ideas regarding public affairs and eventually form public opinion. It can be a specific place where citizens gather (such as a town hall meeting) or a communication infrastructure where citizens send and receive information and opinions.

The problem, of course, is that a functioning public sphere is necessary for a democratic government to function as it should.

My Social Media Adventure

In 2018, when my social media adventure began, I knew nothing about algorithms, the outrage industry, the dangers of partisan punditry, or ideological filter bubbles. I'd soon get a crash course.

One of my earliest lessons was how easily we can be deceived online. Two anonymous accounts claiming to be lawyers had me believing for a while that they were, in fact, lawyers. They posted about legal matters and offered legal opinions. When I realized they were not lawyers, I confronted each of them privately. One soon deleted his account because he had overreached, made absurd predictions, and imploded. The other is still online pretending to be a lawyer. Faking being a lawyer takes work because he has to read legal stuff and then comment on it. I figure he has been faking it so long now that he probably knows as much as some real lawyers.

I also saw firsthand how the sheer complexity of our legal system can give rise to conspiracy theories. My first "viral" thread on Twitter (back when it was called Twitter) happened in September 2018 when a few Twitter users who were in a panic asked me about a case going to the United States Supreme Court, *Gamble v. US*, which they insisted would expand Trump's pardon powers and therefore undo the special counsel probe into the Russian election interference in the 2016 election.

As President, Trump already had the power to issue pardons for federal crimes, so I did some digging. I found the briefing for the case and read it. It seemed to me that the case had nothing whatsoever to do with the presidential pardon power or the special counsel investigation. The case was about a man in Alabama named Terance Martez Gamble who was convicted of possession of a firearm and sentenced to an Alabama prison. After he was convicted in state court, federal prosecutors sought to charge him with the same crime.

Gamble appealed, arguing that being tried and convicted for the same crime violated the Double Jeopardy Clause of the U.S. Constitution, which states, ". . . nor shall any person be subject for the same offence to be twice put in jeopardy of life or limb . . ."

Unfortunately for Gamble, in 1959, the Supreme Court had affirmed something called the Dual Sovereignty Doctrine. This doctrine holds that because state and federal governments are separate jurisdictions, a person who violates both state and federal laws can be charged in both. Gamble was challenging the constitutionality of the Dual Sovereignty Doctrine and asking the Supreme Court to overturn it.

I could not understand how people leaped from Terance Martez Gamble challenging a double conviction in Alabama to Trump escaping justice in the special counsel probe.

I traced the confusion to an article in *The Atlantic*.

The Atlantic advertises itself as fact-driven and aiming for thoughtful engagement. So, let's look at what happened.

The article included a large, unflattering picture of Trump. That alone might make people think the case was about Trump. However, the language in the lead, "could still have consequences" and "isn't related to the Russia investigation," should have been a clue that the connection was remote and the article contained speculation.

The theory connecting the case to the pardon power was this: *If* the Dual Sovereignty Doctrine was abolished, and *if* Trump or his associates were found to have committed a crime in connection with Russia's attack on the 2016 election, and *if* the crimes could be charged in both federal and state court, and *if* the feds went first, Trump or his associates could only be charged in federal court, and not both federal and state courts. That would "expand" Trump's pardon power because he could then pardon himself or his associates in the only jurisdiction where he could be charged.

That is what I would call a creative legal theory.

The "evidence" presented for why the case "could liberate Trump to pardon his associates" was that Republican Senator Orrin Hatch urged the Supreme Court, in an amicus brief, to overturn the Dual Sovereignty Doctrine. The theory was that if a conservative Senator tried to influence the outcome, it must be good for Trump; therefore, it wasn't really about Gamble serving two sentences. It was about Trump escaping justice.

One problem with that theory is that Hatch was a longtime advocate of criminal justice reform. The argument Hatch made in his amicus brief was that the Dual Sovereignty Doctrine should be overturned because it infringed on liberty and violated the Double Jeopardy Clause. Hatch made a decent argument. Is it really fair for someone to serve two sentences for the same crime? If each sentence, separately, was deemed by the respective legislatures to be appropriate for the crime, surely essentially doubling the punishment would be unjust.

I dug deeper and learned that when Trump critics who were following the special counsel investigation found out about the pardon power, they fretted that Trump might be able to pardon himself for any crimes. Lawyers told them not to worry because, if Trump was found to have committed crimes, he likely also committed state crimes, so he could also be charged with those, for which he could not pardon himself.

So, I could see how the reporter got the idea that the case was about the pardon power. I attributed the error to the sheer complexity of the American legal system.

As a result of the framing that *Gamble v. United States* was about the pardon power, the case got a lot of attention. Other outlets picked up the framing of the story.

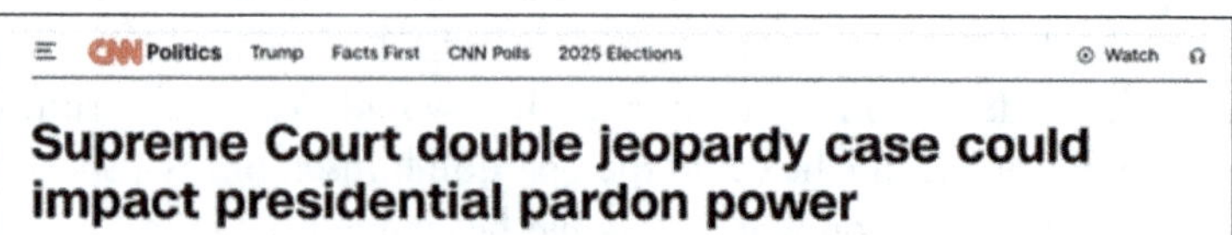

Supreme Court double jeopardy case could impact presidential pardon power

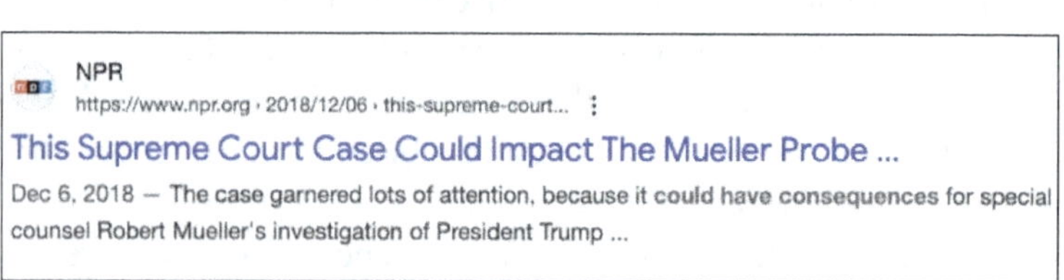

NPR

https://www.npr.org › 2018/12/06 › this-supreme-court...

This Supreme Court Case Could Impact The Mueller Probe ...

Dec 6, 2018 — The case garnered lots of attention, because it could have consequences for special counsel Robert Mueller's investigation of President Trump ...

At the same time this was happening, Brett Kavanaugh was in the process of being confirmed to the Supreme Court. A celebrity who often spoke out against Trump spread the theory that the Republicans were in a hurry to confirm Kavanaugh so he could help Gamble win, which would allow Trump and pals to escape justice. The celebrity posted this to her three million followers on Twitter.

> This is why the GOP is so desperate to confirm Kavanaugh. So that they can all receive a get-out-of-jail-free card once their myriad criminal activities are revealed... like, say, allowing Russia to hack our elections.
>
> On next month's SCOTUS docket is Gamble vs US. No 17-646. This is what the rush is about. Yes,

She deleted the post later when she understood she was wrong. I took a screenshot before she deleted it. I also removed her name.

I won't stop to point out the problems with the facts and logic in her post. I'll just note that others who picked up the idea that there was a nefarious plot to give Trump's associates a get-out-of-jail-free-card said things like this: "The system is unfair! Rich powerful guys get off the hook while poor people get sent to prison for lesser crimes!" The irony is that these same critics were hoping that Mr. Gamble, a guy in Alabama who was decidedly not a privileged billionaire, would have to serve two sentences on the outside chance that this would hurt Trump or his associates.

I responded to the panic by writing a Twitter thread explaining why *Gamble v. United States* wasn't about the pardon power and why, even if there were crimes to charge Trump and his associates with, it was unlikely to impact the special counsel's investigation.

My thread, of course, did nothing to allay the panic, so I tried something bigger. I coauthored a piece for *Slate* with Fordham law professor Jed Shugerman explaining the same thing. As you would expect, our article also did nothing to allay the panic. You cannot put out a forest fire with a squirt gun.

As it turned out, Gamble lost and would have to face prosecution for the same crime in federal court. Kavanaugh, along with five other Justices, voted to uphold the Dual Sovereignty Doctrine. In other words, Justice Kavanaugh didn't vote the way (according to the current theory) that would help Trump. That's because the case wasn't about Trump. It was about Gamble and the Dual Sovereignty Doctrine. Justices Ruth Bader Ginsburg and Neil Gorsuch dissented. They agreed with Orrin Hatch that the Dual Sovereignty Doctrine was fundamentally unfair and undermined the Double Jeopardy Clause. So you see, people don't always fit into the expected boxes.

The idea that Republicans were secretly working in the shadows to expand Trump's pardon power so he could pardon himself and escape justice in the special counsel investigation meets the requirements for a conspiracy theory as described by Professor Young.

Left-Wing and Right-Wing
Conspiracy Theories

Now I'll show you other examples of left-wing and right-wing rage-media-generated conspiracy theories. Remember, a conspiracy theory doesn't need to be unhinged or absurd. It simply needs to falsely assign blame for a confusing situation, and the blame must be assigned to powerful people working in the shadows.

I'll randomly take all examples from the same week in March 2024.

On March 25, 2024, we learned that a New York appellate court, in a case called *New York v. Trump,* reduced Trump's bond from $454 million to $175 million.

The lower court had found Trump liable for inflating his net worth on financial statements over the course of a decade to secure better loans and insurance deals. Trump appealed. To postpone paying the penalty while the case was on appeal, he was required to post a bond. Trump told the court that securing the cash to cover a $454 million bond was a "practical impossibility" and he could not do it. His lawyers argued that "a bond of this size is rarely if ever seen. In the unusual circumstance that a bond of this size is issued, it is provided to the largest public companies in the world, not to individuals or privately held businesses."

The court lowered the bond amount and gave Trump ten days to secure the bond.

A bond is not intended to be a punishment. It is intended to prevent the winning party from executing the judgment while the appeal is pending. Several well-known pundits confirmed for cable audiences that what the court did when it reduced his bond amount was not uncommon. Here is what factual news reporting would look like:

> Donald Trump claimed that securing the cash to cover the bond amount was a "practical impossibility" and unusually large for a case like this one. The appeals court reduced the amount Trump must pay as bond from $450 million to $175 million—and gave him an additional ten days to post it.

MSNBC legal expert Tristan Snell responded with "This is so infuriating, I don't even care what the process is, how the judge arrived at this. I just know it is flawed." Snell then said he agrees with someone else, who implied that Trump is getting special treatment because of who he is. Snell said that Trump "gets his own private court of justice. He has a private plane. He has private clubs that he lives in. He basically fashioned his own private militia to try to take over the Capitol. Now he gets his own system of justice. This is an absolute travesty."

He then said that anyone except Trump who claimed not to have the cash would be told, "Sorry, buddy, you lost. Pay up."

It seems to me that if that were true, if a person who couldn't afford the bond could not appeal, it would mean that only wealthy people would be permitted to appeal large judgments.

What Snell offered was an angry tirade implying that the court, behind the scenes, was behaving unethically. In real life, of course, lawyers are always having rants about what courts do. But this isn't news. It's a personal rant. The problem is that people listening to Snell on MSNBC may take what he says as truth instead of an angry rant that the judge didn't do what Snell wanted the judge to do.

If the measure of success is riling the audience, I give him a high grade. Just listening to his tirade, which I'd certainly characterize as an emotionally evocative performance, made me feel tense and angry. His audience would certainly feel a righteous anger.

Snell posted this on X:

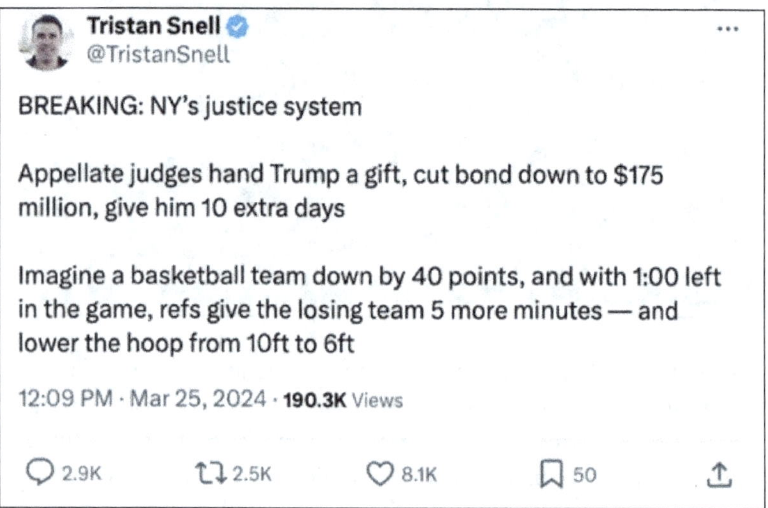

Notice the attempt at humor. What is "breaking" is the New York justice system. The implication is that the courts are cheating on Trump's behalf.

The response meets the criteria for a conspiracy theory as described by Dannagal Goldthwaite Young. Something happened that appears "inexplicable." *Trump's bond was lowered!* People look for a way to assign blame. *The courts are corrupt!* The audience feels part of a group of like-minded outraged citizens. I glanced at a few of the comments on Snell's post, and people were absolutely outraged by this horrible, terrible miscarriage of justice.

It seems to me that, among other things, there is a potential problem here with burnout. If there is an earth-shattering crisis every day, won't some people get numb to it?

The counterintuitive part is that some people will become addicted to the rage. Neuroscientists tell us that this kind of rage feels good because it confirms the biases of the audience and allows them to get behind a banner. They feel in control. They will tune in tomorrow for more, which drives up ratings. We can call it, "enraging people for fun and profit."

Here is another example from the same day in March of 2024. The story began a few weeks earlier in a different case, *The People of the State of New York v. Donald J. Trump,* more commonly known as the hush money case. What happened was this: Trump's legal team claimed that the prosecution dumped tens of thousands of documents on them at the last minute as part of a "strategy to hide the truth." Trump's legal team therefore asked for an extension for an upcoming deadline. On March 14, 2024, the court agreed to a thirty-day extension of time to assess Trump's claim.

Factual reporting would look like this:

> Trump claimed that, because of a last-minute document dump, he could not meet his deadline. In response, the court agreed to a thirty-day extension to assess Trump's claims.

If a network has hours of time to fill, that would obviously not be enough.

Before I show you the spin, hype, and a conspiracy theory, I'll tell you how the story ends. On March 25, after the court had a chance to assess the alleged discovery document dump, Judge Merchan found that Trump and his lawyers misrepresented the facts and that there were no errors on the part of the prosecutors.

The judge, who was visibly angry at Trump's team, said: "It's incredibly serious, unbelievably serious. You are literally accusing the Manhattan District Attorney's office and the people involved in this case of prosecutorial misconduct and trying to make me complicit in it."

On March 14, when Trump was given his extension, before

anyone had any facts, Andrew Weissman, a lawyer, appeared on an MSNBC show.

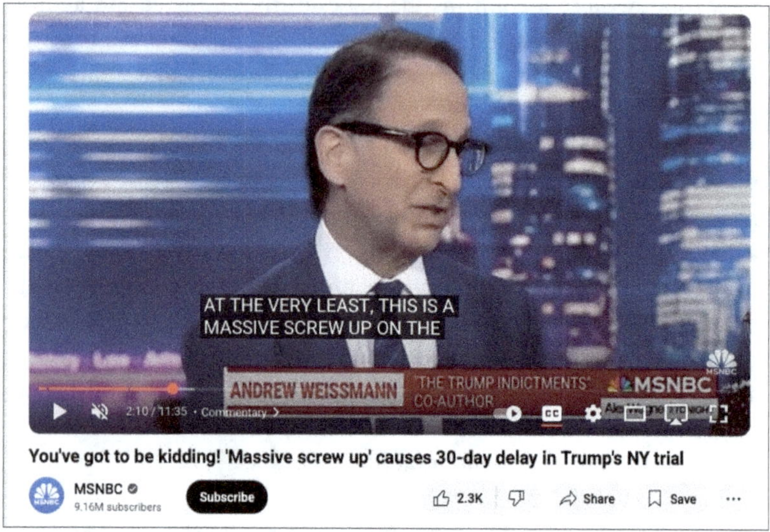

You've got to be kidding! 'Massive screw up' causes 30-day delay in Trump's NY trial

The banner announced "The Justice Delay." The headline offers an emotional quotation from Weissman, "You've got to be kidding!"

The host opened by presenting Trump's claims of a document dump as if it were true, even though she didn't know. She then implied that the prosecutors screwed up. She asked legal expert Andrew Weissman, "What is going on?" He spoke firmly and decisively when he responded with, "At the very least, this is a massive screw-up on the part of the Southern District of New York prosecutors." He accused the SDNY prosecutors of "poor judgment."

Melissa Murray, who is also a lawyer, appeared on the show. She blamed U.S. Attorney General Merrick Garland for the screw-up, even though we find out later that there was never a screw-up.

This, too, is a conspiracy theory. These two legal experts leaped to the conclusion that the prosecutors had screwed up. They falsely assigned blame for something that seemed inexplicable, a last-minute document dump.

When the facts came out, I checked the social media feeds of both Melissa Murray and Andrew Weissman to see if they apologized for their errors. I found no apology or admission of error. They were on to the next outrage. In this new world of outrage media, nobody admits error. There is no collective memory in an ideological filter bubble. Members of the audience come and go. The people who remain are already on to the next outrage.

I have observed that when social media political influencers are wrong about something, they respond by changing the subject and posting content that affirms the biases of their audiences. That keeps them from losing credibility.

I have also observed that, when confronted with contradictory facts, people in ideological filter bubbles find ways to dismiss the evidence, like this: "Okay, maybe the prosecutors didn't screw up this time, but they're always screwing up, which is why Trump gets away with everything, so it wasn't *really* a lie."

Keith M. Bellizzi, a professor of human development, explains why, when it comes to politics, new facts often do not change people's minds. A challenge to a person's worldview may feel like an attack, which can cause that person's views to harden. Cognitive bias kicks in when people encounter evidence that contradicts their firmly held views. Instead of reevaluating their beliefs, they reject the new evidence.

Now, here is an example of a right-wing conspiracy theory.

On March 26, 2024, at 1:28 a.m., the Francis Scott Key Bridge across the Patapsco River in Maryland collapsed. Six members of a maintenance crew who were working on the roadway were killed. Two more were rescued from the river.

When the bridge collapsed, the public had no information. A preliminary report from the National Transportation Safety Board several weeks after the accident indicated that a container ship lost power and drifted into a support pier, triggering a catastrophic chain reaction that led to the collapse.

Immediately after the bridge collapsed, before the public had any information, Anthony Sabatini, a Republican who served in the Florida House of Representatives, posted a response on social media.

DEI stands for diversity, equity, and inclusion. The implication, of course, is that the bridge collapsed because unqualified people were hired because of their race.

Fox News personality Maria Bartiromo mused that the "wide-open border" was responsible for the bridge collapse. She blamed President Joe Biden's immigration policies.

Matt Schlapp on Newsmax said the bridge collapsed because of "drug-addled" employees and COVID lockdowns.

Sabatini's "DEI" post is still online. I assume that it doesn't seem like a lie to people who reason that "it *could* be the result of DEI" or "it is likely the result of DEI" or "even if DEI didn't cause *this*, we know it causes lots of damage." In other words, the lie can be explained away as pointing to what people might think of as a larger truth.

From these examples, you might conclude that the right wing does it better. The right-wing conspiracy theory is more simply stated and more graphically presented. It is also clear what the right-wing pundits hoped to gain. They dislike immigration, DEI as a policy, and COVID lockdowns. Blaming the things you dislike for anything that goes wrong achieves the goal of making other people hate the things you dislike. That, in turn, furthers the goals of a platform that wants to curtail immigration and end DEI hiring.

The left-wing conspiracy theories are more subtle and less graphic. Second-guessing a court's decision and suggesting that the courts are corrupt, that Trump gets preferential treatment, or that the prosecutors screwed up is much less direct. It is also unclear to me what the left-wing gains by attacking the legal system as corrupt. Do they really want Americans to hate the legal system? Does turning people against the legal system benefit liberal policies?

My conclusion is that MSNBC pundits needed a compelling story, and anything related to Trump interests viewers. Accusing the prosecutors who indicted him of screwing up engages and riles the audience.

I am not suggesting that the left wing needs to get better at this. I am suggesting that consumers of news need to see through what is happening. The partisan pundit model is making people less informed and angrier, which risks pushing people into ideological thinking and extremism.

It's easy to see where this is leading. Rage merchants are pushing two groups of angry hyper-partisans to the level of mutual intolerance that (1) endangers democratic forms of government and (2) can lead people to justify cruelty.

Toward a More Enlightened Tomorrow

The issues I've covered can be summarized like this:

- The world has recently undergone rapid changes. The United States government and legal system have grown increasingly complex. The economy is global.

- The very complexity of globalism and our legal system generates conspiracy theories because people look for simple explanations to explain what seems incomprehensible, and so much seems incomprehensible.

- A great many people are malleable and will believe what authorities tell them is true. In our age of fragmented news media, "authorities" often include talk radio stars, cable news pundits, and anyone with a social media account who speaks with enough authority.

- We are in the grip of an information revolution that is causing misinformation, rage, and panic to be disseminated at dangerous levels.

- Our technology is outpacing our wisdom to manage it, which is creating more panic.

- All this is causing a rise in extremist movements.

- Meanwhile, the angriest voices are setting the tone for politics.

In the best of circumstances, democratic forms of government are difficult because they require a lot from the people. Globalism and the complex problems of a large, sprawling, multicultural democracy require that we engage the higher, more evolved parts of our brains rather than the primal ones.

Okay, so *how?*

I'll begin with what doesn't work. If someone is trapped in an ideological filter bubble, calling the person names will not help. I suspect that no one has ever stopped being deluded because someone said, "You are deluded."

Understanding the minds of other men and women and hence embracing the spirit of liberty includes understanding what is happening to those who have been pulled into ideological spirals or who have had their authoritarian impulses activated.

Professor Keith Bellizzi, offers this advice:

> Presenting new things in a nonconfrontational way allows people to evaluate new information without feeling attacked.

> Insulting others and suggesting someone is ignorant or misinformed, no matter how misguided their beliefs may be, will cause the people you are trying to influence to reject your argument. Instead, try asking questions that lead the person to question what they believe. While opinions may not ultimately change, the chance of success is greater.

Karen Stenner reminds us that those with authoritarian vulnerabilities are simple-minded avoiders of complexity—and they are malleable. If one side makes them feel reassured and united by emphasizing shared values, and another side mocks them and makes them feel inadequate, they will transfer their loyalty to the side that offers them a sense of unity. It might seem obvious, but if you want a productive political discussion, start by finding a common cause with people and avoid directly attacking their views. Affirm as much as you can.

Another tactic I have found effective is to say, "The divide isn't left versus right. It's the extremists on either end versus people who are more balanced." I suspect this works because nobody thinks of themselves as an extremist. Everyone believes they are balanced. The extremists are over there. The reasonable people are here.

Reject Rage Merchants

Don't contribute to the noise. Avoid toxic online spaces. The ideal response is to filter out the noise and engage with politics in a more productive way.

Recall that a public reaction against yellow journalism in the late nineteenth century led to a new kind of journalism that was fact-based. This needs to happen again. The more people become aware of what is happening, the sooner such a public reaction can come. Be part of the reaction against this new and improved form of yellow journalism.

Find news outlets that stick to facts. A reader asked me to recommend good sources for news. I can't do that because the moment I recommend a good source, something will change. The only solution is for consumers of news to become sensitive to reporting that is not factual.

Good reporters are necessary to a functioning democracy. Find ways to support reporters who stick to the facts. You can be sure that their social media comments are filled with angry partisans who don't like their attempts at neutrality.

We must insist on non-partisan news reporting that engages the more evolved parts of our brains. If something enrages you, look to see what reasonable people with alternative viewpoints are saying and ask yourself why they are saying whatever it is. This will better enable you to discuss issues with people who disagree with you.

Just as the printing press caused people to be inundated with large quantities of material that they were not equipped to evaluate, people today are being bombarded via the Internet with material that they are not equipped to evaluate, including AI-generated or deep fakes. People need a new set of tools to evaluate online sources.

When you want to feel riveted or captivated, turn to the arts, not partisan pundits.

Withhold Judgment as Long as You Can

When I taught college English, I noticed that many of my students were quick to judge literary characters, but slow to sympathize with them. I thought this was a problem. I agreed with John Updike, who said the purpose of literature is to enlarge our sympathies.

There is an abundance of ways to enlarge our sympathies that help us become more flexible and nuanced thinkers. The study of literature is one way. The towering literary figures endure because they reveal essential truths about human nature. Shakespeare understood the authoritarian personality and ideological spirals long before the phrases were coined. If you don't believe me, read *Julius Caesar* and pay attention to the behavior of the crowds. Read *Richard III* and notice how easily the citizens and noblemen accept Richard as their savior against supposed threats.

The study of history is another way. History offers perspective and shows that there is more than one way forward. When we look back and study what has been, we understand the wisdom in King Solomon's words in Ecclesiastes 1:9: "What has been is what will be, and what has been done is what will be done, and there is nothing new under the sun."

I found that the work of a criminal defense lawyer is also good practice for withholding judgment and trying to understand the minds of men and women. The job of the defense lawyer is to say things such as, "Let's look more closely at the facts," and "Let's consider what happened from the viewpoint of the defendant."

The question defense lawyers often get is "But what if they're guilty?" Another—and perhaps a better—question is this: "But what if they're not?"

Don't Become Cynical

Both life and democracy are difficult. Cynicism comes from expecting these things to be easy and then giving up when discovering that they are not easy. Those who do not want to confront the difficulty of both life and democracy are vulnerable to the siren call of a demagogue who promises easy answers.

Democracy requires work, and that cannot happen when people give in to hopelessness, cynicism, or panic. Of the three, panic is the most dangerous. After spending time on social media, I concluded that if I wanted to enable autocracy, I would find a way to keep people in a state of constant panic. Panic impairs rational thought, wears people out, and makes them more likely to commit desperate acts that add to the confusion and chaos.

Make Politics Cool Again

Plato's concern for democracy was that too few people can think deeply about the complex issues inherent in politics. He also believed that people were too susceptible to demagoguery for democracy to be stable. But if, as Karen Stenner tells us, one-third of the population is "simple-minded avoiders of complexity," then two-thirds remain who should be able to think about the complex issues that politics involves.

Currently, the loud, angry, hyper-partisans dominate the conversation, drowning out more nuanced perspectives and shaping the way we think about politics. The non-extremists must find a way to re-establish a shared factuality and set a new tone for discussing politics.

It's time for the rest of us—the majority—to reclaim the public sphere.

There is a wonderful passage in historian Doris Kearns Goodwin's book, *Team of Rivals* about the Lincoln era and how, in the nineteenth century, politics was a concern to all citizens. She opens Chapter Three, "The Lure of Politics," with this image from Noah Webster's *Elementary Spelling Book*, which was widely read in Abraham Lincoln's time:

And this:

> In the only country founded on the principle that men should and could govern themselves, where self-government dominated every level of human association from the smallest village to the nation's capital, it was natural politics should be a consuming, almost universal concern.

A cave-dweller with a philosophical frame of mind who heard the approach of a predatory cat and stopped to consider all possible responses while contemplating the point of view of the cat would most likely be lunch meat. Parts of our brains are still in the "watch for predatory animals" stage of evolution. This creates more problems than it solves because we now live in a world of the Internet and a global economy. Our technology is in danger of outpacing our wisdom to handle it. Meanwhile, we are generally not in danger of predatory cats. We are, however, in danger of facts being lost in a tidal wave of speculation, spin, and conspiracy theories and reacting to those with our most primal emotions.

The best response to any political situation, therefore, is to pause, delve more deeply into the facts, and think about the best response.

Notes

1: Demagogues and Artists

3. "Chileans, who had long prided … succumbed to dictatorship." Levitsky and Ziblatt, *How Democracies Die*, p. 116.
5. "ruled harshly but left behind the most successful country in Latin America." Packenham and Ratliff, The Hoover Institution, "What Pinochet Did for Chile," January 30, 2007.
5. "I think Pinochet . . . dreamer and even a visionary." *The Washington Independent Review of Books*, September 9, 2015.
7. "Friend . . . Well, ya got trouble, my friend." *The Music Man*, Meredith Wilson.
8. "Golden rule of democracies." Eli Merritt, "Civics 101: Keep Demagogues Out of Democracy." The Vanderbilt Project on Unity and Democracy, available here: https://www.vanderbilt.edu/unity/
9. "intolerance of ambiguity." Theodor W. Adorno, Else Frenkel-Brunswik, Daniel Levinson, and Nevitt Sanford. *The Authoritarian Personality*, 325.
9. "oneness and sameness." *Hope Not Hate*, January 11, 2020.
10. "Difference-ism . . . avoiders of complexity . . . another way to be human." Ibid.
10. "punitiveness toward dissidents and deviants." Ibid.
10. "not a fundamental and enduring dimension of human nature." Ibid.
11. "Societies seem to thrive when there's a balanced mix of folks who monitor the boundaries and guard against the strange and unfamiliar, and others who seek out novelty and variety." Ibid.
16. "the style of thinking characterized by rigid adherence to a

dogma and a rigid social identity." *The Ideological Brain: The Radical Science of Flexible Thinking*,13.

17. "The spirit of liberty . . . minds of other men and women." Learned Hand, "The Spirit of Liberty," 1944,

18. "In a given community . . . to come out." Zmigrod, *The Ideological Brain: The Radical Science of Flexible Thinking*, 201.

18. "The spiral reflects . . . ideological environment." Ibid. 199.

19. "pain that is always there . . immortality itself." Yalom, *Love's Executioner,* 3.

22. "Where, if not from the impressionists . . . exaggerated and over-emphasized." Wilde, "The Decay of Lying," 1913.

23. Coleridge, Specimens of the Table Talk of Samuel Taylor Coleridge, 1836.

23-24. "One of the most sublime . . . of all time." Hegel, *Lectures on Aesthetics*, 464.

26. "The world will be saved by beauty." Dostoevsky, *The Idiot.* Available here: https://www.gutenberg.org/ebooks/2638

2: These are the Times that Try Men's Souls

27. "All times . . . became common." Edelman, *The Symbolic Uses of Politics*, 13.

28. "*Zenger Trial.*" To read more about the Zenger Trial, see: https://terikanefield.com/juries-and-the-zenger-trial/

31. "2,500 or more was 5.1%," U.S. Census Bureau.

31. "4% of colonists," "Read the Revolution," Museum of the American Revolution.

32. "80% of Americans," U.S. Census Newsroom, "Redefining Urban Areas."

32. "40% of Americans," Pew Research Center, "Religious Landscape Study."

30. "71% of the electorate." Pew Research Center, "Demographics of Trump and Harris Voters," available on the Pew Research

Center website.

32-33. "Christian nationalism . . . preserve our cultural identity." *Christianity Today*, "What is Christian Nationalism?"

32. "All persons . . . shall be freely tolerated." 1778 South Carolina Constitution.

37-38. "That God designed . . . exceptional cases," *Bradwell v. The State*, 83, U.S. 16 (1872).)

39. "Woman's sustenance . . . his power over her," *Harper, Life and Work*, vol. 1, 231.)

44. "Yeah, that's here . . . You can do anything." *Access Hollywood*, available here: https://www.bbc.com/news/election-us-2016-37595321

45. "Hey there . . . a big bad wolf would want." Lyrics, Sam the Sham, *Red Riding Hood*. Available on YouTube.

46. "The militia may be here destroyed . . . by disarming them," Waldman, *The Second Amendment: A Biography*, 46.

46. "ultimate safety . . . detested everywhere." Waldman, Waldman, *The Second Amendment: A Biography*, 38.

47. "A little rebellion . . . a good thing," Thomas Jefferson to James Madison, January 30, 1787.

48. "Republican extremism . . taken from them," Levitsky and Way, "America's Coming Age of Instability."

3. The Appeal of Autocracy

49. "charismatic leader," Weber, "Politics as a Vocation."

50. "59% of Americans . . . disapproved," Gallup Vault, "Americans Narrowly OK'd 1964 Civil Rights Law.

53. "Democracy is messy. Authoritarianism is neat," Swan, Michael, "Protect Messy Spirit of Ukraine's Democracy."

56. " If men were angels, no government would be necessary," *The Federalist Papers* 51.

62. "replied stubbornly. . . stay in," Andrea Most, "You've Got to

be Carefully Taught."

62.   "underlying philosophy . . . Moscow," Ibid.

62.   "It's not born in you . . . carefully taught," *South Pacific*, Rodgers and Hammerstein.

62.   "Life is difficult . . . no longer matters." Peck, *The Road Less Traveled*, 1.

4. Rage Merchants

68.   "Media producers sought . . . as wide a swath as possible," Young, *Wrong! How Media, Politics and Identity Drive Our Appetite for Misinformation, 172.* 70. "I happen to have great entertainment skills," Chafets, *The New York Times*, July 6, 2008.

70.   "Feminism was established . . . Jesse Jackson?" Zurcher, BBC, February 17, 2021. Available here: https://www.bbc.com/news/world-us-canada-56105331

71-72. "The phenomenon of the Partisan Pundit . . this seems to be the case," Young, *Wrong!* p. 144 - 145.

74.   "minute-by-minute rating data," *New York Times*, Confessore, Nicholas. "What to Know About Tucker Carlson's Rise."

75.   "85% of MSNBC . . . 54% factual reporting," Jurkowitz, "Is MSNBC the Place for Opinion?"

75.   "As partisan political views . . . merely has opinions," Ciciora, *Illinois News Bureau*.

76.   "respectively 67, 68, and 71," Shafer, Jack "Old People Love Cable News -- and They Vote," *Politico*.

76.   "Conspiracy theories . . . public in the dark." Young, *Wrong! How Media, Politics and Identity Drive Our Appetite for Misinformation*" 42.

77.   "Our date indicates . . . even nastier." Sobieraj and Berry, *The Other Divide*, 42).

78.   "132,000 prime time viewers . . . 2.2 million viewers." Patten,

Deadline, "MSNBC Ratings Crater to All-Time Lows, Fox News Tops Q1 Results, CNN Up." See also: See also Adweek, available here: https://www.adweek.com/tvnewser/2020-ratings-msnbc-sets-network-records-ranks-no-2-in-total-viewers-but-no-3-among-adults-25-54/

79. "May not be good for America . . . CBS." Moonves, *Politico,* February 29, 2016.

5. Social Media Makes it Worse

80. "Often . . . sometimes." Pew Research Center, "Social Media Fact Sheet.

81. "The Pew Research Center has found . . . rather by algorithms." Available here: https://www.pewresearch.org/internet/2018/11/16/algorithms-in-action-the-content-people-see-on-social-media/

82. "angry content," Zubrow, "Facebook Whistleblower Says Company Incentivizes Angry, Polarizing, Divisive Content."

82. "Daily Wire . . . (D-NY)." Platformer, available here: https://www.platformer.news/the-secret-list-of-twitter-vips-getting/

83. "tightly controlled propagandist state . . . radicalizing spaces," Zmigrod, *The Ideological Brain,* 222.

90. "A bond of this size . . . privately held business," Rushe and Aratani, *The Guardian,* "Trump Civil Fraud Case."

91. "This is so infuriating," clip available here: x.com/TPostMillennial/status/1772297738928988164

93. "It's incredibly serious, unbelievably serious . . . trying to make me complicit in it," Italiano, L., "Judge Scolds Trump Lawyer." Available here: https://www.businessinsider.com/trump-lawyer-scolded-bigly-after-botched-hush-money-delay-bid-2024-3. See also *Lawfare*'s reporting on the hearing: https://www.lawfaremedia.org/article/a-trial-date-certain-ish-ny-trump-case-set-to-begin-april-15#:~:text=Merchan%20

now%20comes%20to%20page,defendant's%20efforts%20
to%20obtain%20evidence."

94. "The Justice Delay," clip available here: https://x.com/
WagnerTonight/status/1768749117377847335

96. "Wide-open border ... drug addled." "Unfounded Conspiracy
Theories Spread Online after Baltimore Bridge Collapse,"
NBC News, available here: https://www.nbcnews.com/tech/
francis-scott-key-bridge-collapse-conspiracy-theories-online-
rcna145105

Toward a More Enlightened Tomorrow

99. "Presenting new thigs . . . chance of success is greater," Bellizzi,
"Cognitive Biases and Brain Biology Help Explain Why Facts
Don't Change Minds."

103. "In the only country . . almost universal concern," Goodwin,
Team of Rivals, 60.

Bibliography

Books

Theodor W. Adorno, Else Frenkel-Brunswik, Daniel Levinson, and Nevitt Sanford. *The Authoritarian Personality.* Harper, 1950.

Amar, Akhil Reed. *The Bill of Rights: Creation and Reconstruction.* Yale University Press, 2001.

Anderson, Carol. *The Second Amendment: Race and Guns in a Fatally Unequal America.* Bloomsbury Publishing, 2021.

Arendt, Hannah, *Eichmann in Jerusalem: A Report on the Banality of Evil.* Viking (revised and enlarged edition). 1977.

Brownmiller, Susan. *Against our Will: Men, Women, and Rape.* Ballantine Books. Ballantine Books, 1993.

Coolidge, Samuel Taylor. *Specimens of the Table Talk of Samuel Taylor Coleridge,* 1836.

Edelman, Murray. *The Symbolic Uses of Politics*, University of Illinois Press, Chicago. 1967.

Ferling, John. *A Leap in the Dark.* Oxford University Press, 2003.

Gessen, Masha. *The Future is History: How Totalitarianism Reclaimed Russia.* Riverhead Books, 2017

Haidt, Jonathan. *The Righteous Mind: Why Good People are Divided by Politics and Religion.* Pantheon, 2012.

Harper, Ida Husted. *The Life and Work of Susan B. Anthony,* Indianapolis: Bowen-Merril, 1899.)

Hegel's Aesthetics. Lectures on Fine Art, translated by T.M. Knox.

Goodwin, Doris Keans. *Team of Rivals.* Simon and Schuster, 2005.

Krupnikov, Yanna and John Ryan. *The Other Divide.* Cambridge University Press, 2022

Magyar, Balint. *Post-Communist Mafia State: The Case of Hungary.* Central European University Press, 2016.

Mercieca, Jennifer *Demagogue for President: The Rhetorical Genius of Donald Trump.* Texas A&M University Press,

Pariser, Eli. *The Filter Bubble: What the Internet is Hiding from You.* Penguin Press, 2011.

Peck, Scott. *The Road Less Traveled.* Touchstone Books, 1978.

Richardson, Heather Cox. *How the South Won the Civil War.* Oxford University Press, 2020.

Sarah Sobieraj and Jeffrey Berry. *The Outrage Industry: Public Opinion Media and the New Incivility.* Oxford University Press, 2016.

Sophocles. *Antigone.*

Stenner, Karen. *The Authoritarian Dynamic.* Cambridge University Press, 2005.

Waldman, Michael. *The Second Amendment: A Biography.* Simon and Schuster, 2015.

Yalom, Irvin D. *Love's Executioner.* Basic Books, 1989.

Young, Dannagal Goldthwaite. *Wrong! How Media, Politics and Identity Drive Our Appetite for Misinformation.* Hopkins Press, 2023.

Zmigrod, Leor. *The Ideological Brain: The Radical Science of Flexible Thinking,* Henry Holt and Co., 2025.

Ziblatt, Levitsky. *How Democracies Die.* Crown, *2018*

Articles and Essays

"An Interview with Marjorie Agosín," *The Washington Independent Review of Books,* September 9, 2015.

Arenella, Peter, "The Perils of TV Legal Punditry," *The University of Chicago Legal Forum,* vol. 1998, Issue 1, page 3.

Bellizzi, Keith M., "Cognitive Biases and Brain Biology Help Explain Why Facts Don't Change Minds," *UConn Today,* August 16, 2025.

Phil Ciciora, Illinois News Bureau, Study: Americans Struggle to Distinguish Factual Claims from Opinions Amid Partisan Bias.

Chafets, Zev, "Late-Period Limbaugh," *The New York Times,* July 6, 2008.

Confessore, Nicholas. "What to Know About Tucker Carlson's Rise." *The New York Times,* 30 Apr. 2022.

"Demographics of Trump and Harris Voters," Pew Research Center, available on the Pew Research Center website.

Hand, Learned, "The Spirit of Liberty," 1944.

Gallup Vault: Americans Narrowly OK'd 1964 Civil Rights Law," available on the Gallup website.

Jurkowitz, Mark, "Is MSNBC the Place for Opinion?" Pew Research Center, June 5, 2013.

Thomas Jefferson to James Madison, January 30, 1787, available on the Founders Online website.

Italiano, L., "Judge Scolds Trump Lawyer," *Business Insider*, March 25, 2024.

Kanai, Ryota, and Tom Feilden, Colin Firth, Geraint Rees, "Political Orientations are Correlated with Brain Structure in Young Adults," *Current Biology*, April 7, 2011.

Levitsky, Steven and Lucan Way, "America's Coming Age of Instability," *Foreign Affairs*, January 20, 2022.

Merritt, Eli, "Civics 101: Keep Demagogues Out of Democracy," The Vanderbilt University Project on Unity and American Democracy.

Most, Andrea, "You've Got to Be Carefully Taught": The Politics of Race in Rodgers and Hammerstein's South Pacific, *Theatre Journal*, 52 (2000) 307-337.

Miller, Paul, D. "What is Christian Nationalism?" *Christianity Today*, February 3, 2021.

Packenham, Robert A. and William Ratliff, The Hoover Institution, *What Pinochet Did for Chile*, January 30, 2007.

Patten, Dominic, "MSNBC Ratings Crater to All-Time Lows, Fox News Tops Q1 Results, CNN Up," *Deadline*, March 31, 2015.

"Read the Revolution," Museum of the American Revolution, here: https://www.amrevmuseum.org/read-the-revolution/reading-list-the-role-of-cities-in-the-american-revolution

"Redefining Urban Areas Following the 2020 Census," United States Census Bureau, available on the US Census Bureau website.

"Religious Landscape Study," Pew Research Center, available on the Pew Research Center website.

Rushe, Dominic and Lauren Aratani, "Trump Civil Fraud Case." *The Guardian*, March 25, 2024.

Schiffer, Zoe, "The Secret List of Twitter VIPs Getting Boosted Over Everyone Else," *The Platformer,* March 27, 2023.

Shafer, Jack "Old People Love Cable News -- and They Vote," *Politico.*

Sparks, Brandon, Alexandra Zidenberg, and Mark Oliver, "Involuntary Celibacy: A Review of Incel Ideology and Experiences with Dating, Rejection, and Associated Mental Health and Emotional Sequelae," *Current Psychiatry Reports,* November 17, 2022.

"Social Media Fact Sheet," *Pew Research Center,* September 25, 2025.

Stenner, Karen "Authoritarianism," *Hope Not Hate,* January 11, 2020.

Stenner, Karen and Jonathan Haidt, "The Authoritarian Personality," included in *Can it Happen Here: Authoritarianism in America.* Dey Street Books, 2018.

Smith, Aaron, "Algorithms in Action: The Content People See on Social Media," *Pew Research Center,* November 16, 2018.

Swan, Michael, "Protect Messy Spirit of Ukraine's Democracy," *CNG Media,* February 8, 2022.

The Stanford Dictionary of Philosophy, available online.

United States Census Bureau, "Increasing Urbanization: Population Distribution by City Size, 1790-1890."

Weber, Max, "Politics as a Vocation," from Max Weber: Essays in Sociology, translated and edited by H.H. Gerth and C. Wright Mills, 1919.

Wilde, Oscar, "The Decay of Lying," 1913.

Zubrow, Keith, "Facebook Whistleblower Says Company Incentivizes "Angry, Polarizing, and Divisive Content," CBC news, October 4, 2021.

Zurcher, Anthony, BBC, February 17, 2021.

Cases Cited or Mentioned

Bradwell v. The State, 83 U.S. 130 (1872)

Brown v. Board of Education, 347 U.S. 483 (1954).

Chambers v. Florida, 309 U.S. 227 (1940).

Dred Scott v. Sanford, 60 U.S. 393 (1856)
Gamble v. United States, 139 S. Ct. 1960 (2019)
Lochner v. New York, 198 U.S. 45 (1905)
New York v. Trump, No. 25-1236 (1st Cir. 2025)
The People of the State of New York v. Donald J. Trump, No. 71543/2023
Plessy v. Ferguson, 163 U.S. 537 (1896)
Roe v. Wade, 410 U.S. 113 (1973)
Smith v. Allwright, 321 U.S. 649 (1944)
State v. A. B. Rhodes, 61 N.C. 453 (1868).

Cable News Clips

"This is so Infuriating," Tristin Snell on MSNBC. Clip available here: x.com/TPostMillennial/status/1772297738928988164

"The Justice Delay," Andrew Weissman and Lisa Murray on MSNBC. https://x.com/WagnerTonight/status/1768749117377847335

Unfounded Conspiracy Theories Spread Online after Baltimore Bridge Collapse," NBC News, clip available here: www.nbcnews.com/tech/francis-scott-key-bridge-collapse-conspiracy-theories-online-rcna145105

Artists and Performers Cited

Ledroit, Stephanie, Paintings can be found on her website. www.StephanieLedroit.com
Munch, Edvard, "The Scream," 1893.
Preston, Robert performing Meredith Wilson's "Ya Got Trouble," 1962.
Sam the Sham performing "Little Red Riding Hood," 1966.

ABOUT THE AUTHOR

Teri Kanefield's books have won numerous awards and distinctions, including the Jane Addams Book Award and the Carter G. Woodson Middle-Level Book Award. *Firehose of Falsehood* was named by the New York Public Library as one of the best new graphic books for adults. Three of her books have been named Junior Library Guild selections. *Rebels, Robbers, and Radicals: The Story of the Bill of Rights* was selected as a Junior Library Guild Gold Standard.

She has written legal commentary for *The Washington Post*, NBC, CNN, and other mainstream outlets. Her short stories and essays have appeared in publications as diverse as *Education Week, The Iowa Review, Cricket Magazine, Scope*, and the *American Literary Review.*

She earned her law degree from the University of California, Berkeley. Her private law practice was limited to representing indigents on appeal from adverse rulings. Before law school, she taught English at the college and university level. She holds an MA in English with an emphasis in fiction writing from the University of California, Davis, and an undergraduate degree from the University of Pennsylvania.

To learn more about Teri and her books, please visit: www.terikanefield.com.